P9-CAO-974

Huskies Write

A Writer's Guide to Composition and College Life

Editor and Text
Rex Veeder

Associate Editor and Design
Jason Tham

St. Cloud State University

FOUNTAINHEAD
PRESS

As a textbook publisher, we are faced with enormous environmental issues due the large amount of paper contained in our print products. Since our inception in 2002, we have worked diligently to be as eco-friendly as possible.

Our "green" initiatives include:

Electronic Products
We deliver products in non-paper form whenever possible. This includes pdf downloadables, flash drives, & CD's.

Electronic Samples
We use a new electronic sampling system, called Xample. Instructor samples are sent via a personalized web page that links to pdf downloads.

FSC Certified Printers
All of our Printers are certified by the Forest Service Council which promotes environmentally and socially responsible management of the world's forests. This program allows consumer groups, individual consumers and businesses to work together hand in hand to promote responsible use of the world's forests as a renewable and sustainable resource.

Recycled Paper
Almost all of our products are printed on a minimum of 10-30% post consumer waste recycled paper.

Support of Green Causes
When we do print, we donate a portion of our revenue to Green causes. Listed below are a few of the organizations that have received donations from Fountainhead Press. We welcome your feedback and suggestions for contributions, as we are always searching for worthy initiatives.
Rainforest 2 Reef
Environmental Working Group

Editor and Text: Rex Veeder
Associate Editor and Design: Jason Tham
Contributing Writers: Amanda Pillatzk, Katelin Moquin, Erin Schaefer, Douglas LeBlanc
Cover Image: University Communications, St. Cloud State University
Cover Design: Jason Tham
Iconic Figures: Kelly Marie Beckius

Copyright © 2013

All rights reserved. No part of this book may be reproduced or utilized in any form or by any means, electronic or mechanical, including photocopying and recording, or by any informational storage and retrieval system, without written permission from the publisher.
Books may be purchased for educational purposes.

For information, please call or write:
1-800-586-0330
Fountainhead Press
Southlake, TX 76092
Website: www.fountainheadpress.com
E-mail: customerservice@fountainheadpress.com

ISBN: 978-1-59871-706-8

Printed in the United States of America

*To the students, faculty, and administration of SCSU and their dedication to creating knowledge — to the community of scholars we enjoy and must nurture. We hope that **Huskies Write** will not only be useful for you in First-Year Composition, but that those who work with it and with us will find it an important book for their entire academic career and, perhaps, after they graduate.*

Participate
Influence
Respect

Preface

Jump in early.

A story repeated every semester in First-Year Composition is that a student dreads taking composition but shows up because he or she has to in order to meet SCSU requirements. The student is balancing changes in address, friends, points of view, financial responsibilities, and academic challenges for the course. From the first day of class, the student tests the waters of the class to see if jumping in is a good idea. Should he or she get involved? Is it dangerous to commit to the class? The student puts a toe in the water to test the temperature. This is a critical moment in the student's career and life since the decision to jump or not makes all the difference. Staying on the bank of a river or on a beach beside an ocean is sometimes relaxing, but it doesn't get us far. At some point, the student either jumps in or watches everyone else get wet and swim and drift away from her or him. The key to all future success or failure is determined by jumping in and embracing the cold water long enough to get used to it.

In our repeated story, the student who jumps in begins to get into a rhythm of going to class, reading, writing, planning, talking, and responding to feedback from classmates and the composition instructor. That rhythm quickly becomes a habit that is satisfying and easily repeated. Journals, notes, drafts of papers, research documentation, composing social media, electronic composing, and final papers are written and evaluated. Social events, conferences and talks, sports, getting to know strangers, and exotic ideas that become familiar — all of these things, too, become a part of the experience of First-Year Composition.

When the semester ends, the students who were once hesitant, and perhaps even fearful or combative, recognize a satisfaction in what was done, what was learned, and what they take with them to the next classes and the next challenges in their lives. In the end, getting into the water with the class is a decision they recognize as one of the best decisions they ever made.

This is a story repeated again and again in First-Year Composition, and a pattern that any student, to one degree or another, follows. As you begin the semester, keep your eye on the prize you will be claiming at semester's end and jump right in.

Welcome

Greetings! I know I speak for my colleagues when I say we are truly honored to welcome you to the English Department. We take the teaching of writing very seriously here, and will do everything we can to ensure your future success at SCSU and beyond.

Dr. Glenn Davis
Chair, Department of English

Welcome to the SCSU First-Year Writing Program! We are pleased that you have chosen to study at St. Cloud State and wish you the best in your study of rhetoric and writing during your first-year writing experience.

Dr. James Heiman
Director of Composition

Contents

Huskies Write

A Writer's Guide to Composition and College Life

ORIENTATION

Simplicity is the ultimate sophistication.

- Leonardo da Vinci

A significant moment in the movie *The Wizard of Oz* is when Dorothy peeks behind a curtain to reveal the Wizard at a panel. He had been creating frightening images representing the Wizard and projecting them on a screen. It's disappointing at first to know the All-Powerful Oz is a human being and that his image is merely effects. On the other hand, those images made him all-powerful, and in the end the Wizard does grant Dorothy and her crew their wishes.

The mystery of writing and talking shop: Peeking behind the curtain.

Consider your class a peek behind a curtain of the powerful and at times frightening world of composition. In a way, if you are taking the class, you are learning to become the Wizard. Many of the assignments, advice, and processes revealed or discussed more fully in **Huskies Write** are our way of drawing back the curtain of mystery with craft talk or shop talk.

To be a shop talker or a workshop participant is to join the club. You get to do what writers or composers do to be social, get their work done, and do their work better. There's nothing mysterious about it. In fact, you have been doing the same sort of thing all your life. A peer review workshop, for example, could be a lot like planning a party since you are trying to organize a performance together. Or, a peer review workshop might be like the gathering of a crew remodeling a home. Workshops are meetings but also impromptu gatherings just like the ones you have attended while at working and playing all your life.

When you engage in these activities in class and out of class, you are a composer, a writer. What follows are questions often asked about composition and specifically about First-Year Composition.

> If there's a book that you want to read, but it hasn't been written yet, then you must write it.
>
> — Toni Morrison

THINKING ALOUD

It's a good idea to invest some time during the semester to work on your skills in terms of workshops and meetings. More than ever, what was considered group work has changed to collaborative and team work. The skill of working this way is a primary skill in academics, science, business, and health care. Imagine a physician who refused to participate in meetings with other physicians or was lazy about her or his contribution. The diagnosis for the patients would be suspect at best.

Questions and answers regarding *Huskies Write* and First-Year Composition

What is First-Year Composition?

First-Year Composition courses at SCSU include ENGL 190, 191, 198, 291 and sections of Honors that meet the criteria of any of those courses. ENGL 190 is a course taught in collaboration with the Write Place. ENGL 198 is a course that fulfills the requirements and focuses on literature and writing. ENGL 291 is designed for transfer students who need to fulfill SCSU's writing requirement.

> The English Department at SCSU describes ENGL 191 as follows: Analytic reading, writing, and critical reasoning for a variety of rhetorical purposes, including argumentation (broadly conceived). Practice in developing ideas, insights, and claims through use of both personal observation/experience and external texts and perspectives. From this workshop-oriented course, you should gain awareness of the composing processes of invention, drafting and revision; the rhetorical concepts of audience and purpose, methods for developing, organizing and editing your writing, and strategies for reading, researching, and analyzing various texts.

Why take a writing class?

A writing class offers an understanding of processes students use for study, thinking, analysis, and interpretation. A writing class offers insights into who we are as individuals and who we are in relation to society and the world. To write is to be engaged with the world. Writing classes explore the art and craft of writing in relation to living in the academic environment as well as other professional environments.

Writing is a social activity dedicated to accomplishing something that is important to those brought together by the activity. Writing is physical, requiring stamina and sweat. Like many social activities writing can be boring or irritating but also exhilarating, as in the times when a writer finds or constructs a combination of skill, topic, and community necessary for doing writing well.

What are the differences between high school and college?

The differences between high school and post secondary (college) environments can be startling for First-Year Composition students, especially if they are coming straight from the high school environment or have never been to college. Based on several reviews and comparisons, what follows is adapted from www.smu.edu/alec/transition.asp.

What to expect in your freshman year

The walk across the stage to receive that long-sought-after high school diploma is over. You and your parents have selected the right college and it is time to leave home to begin your move into a college dorm and your year as a college freshman.

You have prepared for this since the beginning of high school. It will be the beginning of your life as a young adult: instead of reporting in to your parents every day, you will make the decision about you study and when you will socialize. This is your first taste of freedom. However, there is a part of this new personal freedom that has a bit of mystery to it.

What should you expect in your freshman year at college? Generally, the differences between college and high school will fall into the following categories:

- Making responsible choices
- Understanding how to succeed in college classes
- College professors
- Test taking and grades

Making responsible choices begins as soon as you enter your first class. "A student may expect a lot of apparent free time in their first year," says associate professor of chemistry Joseph S. Ward III, PhD. Ward is a coordinator of first-year advising and chief health professions advisor at Rockford College in Illinois.

"Typically a student is in class about 15 hours a week, with sometimes hours between classes. Some students think this is an opportunity to expand upon their partying and social life or maybe take on a job working nearly full time to make extra money."

This is a misconception that becomes clear very soon in the first semester of your freshman year in college. "It is a common rule of thumb that for every hour you are in class, you should spend two hours outside of class," says Ward. "So 15 hours in class and 30 hours outside of class make for a 45-hour week of just classroom-related work. This is more than a full-time job. This is not including special projects and extra studying for exams."

The misconception of free time is just one of the major differences between high school and college. You are generally following rules in high school; when you reach your freshman year in college, you are required to make the right choices independently. According to the article, How College Differs From High School, from Southern Methodist University (SMU) in Texas:

> In high school you can count on parents and teachers to remind you of your responsibilities and to guide you in setting priorities. [In college] you must balance your responsibilities and set priorities. You will face moral and ethical decisions you have never faced before ... In high school most of your classes are arranged for you. [In college] you arrange your own schedule in consultation with your advisor. Schedules tend to look lighter than they really are ... High school guiding principle: You will usually be told what to do and corrected if your behavior is out of line. [College] guiding principle: You are expected to take responsibility for what you do and don't do, as well as for the consequences of your decisions.

As a high school student, if you attended regularly and made an effort to do minimal homework and participate, you could expect reasonable success. In high school, even if you did not complete the reading assignments, the material would usually be discussed in class the next day.

The requirements for college success are vastly different from those for high school, however. Attending on a regular basis is not enough. The SMU article points out the following college requirements:

- You need to study at least two to three hours outside of class for each hour spent in class.
- You need to review class notes and reading material regularly.
- You are assigned substantial amounts of reading and writing which may not be directly addressed in class.

- It's up to you to read and understand the assigned material; lectures and assignments proceed from the assumption that you've already done so.
- Classes may number 100 students or more.

High school teachers and college professors are both interested in teaching, but the approach to teaching is very different. The differences may come as a shock to college freshmen.

Dr. Drew Appleby, PhD, a professor and director of undergraduate studies in psychology at Indiana University-Purdue University of Indianapolis, gives his students a 16-page syllabus at the beginning of the semester. In his syllabus, Appleby writes:

> Many of the freshmen I teach tell me that their high school teachers taught them what was in their textbooks (i.e., in the words of the ancient ... proverb, 'gave them a fish'). Whereas, their college teachers provide them with an environment in which to learn (i.e. in the words of the ancient ... proverb, 'taught them how to fish'). [College level] teachers assume students are mature and responsible enough to learn by themselves. That is, teachers don't teach students; they create and provide opportunities for their students to learn.

Tests and grading in the freshman year of college are vastly different than in high school. According to Appleby:

> I have found that many of my freshmen expect to be graded on the basis of the effort they expend. They believe they deserve high grades if they work hard, follow their teachers' instructions and complete all assignments, even if they do not perform well on tests or papers. At this stage, students believe the quantity of their work is more important than its quality.
>
> [College level] students slowly begin to understand that their grades will be based on their actual performance on tests and papers, not on the effort they expend studying for their tests or writing their papers. At this later stage, students know and accept that they will be graded on the quality of the products they produce, not simply on the quantity of work they have expended.

Orientation

You will experience many differences in your freshman year at college. Your teachers' expectations may seem great. But by learning how to navigate this year successfully, you will ease the transition to college life and set yourself up for greater success in subsequent years.

Source: www.secure.cfwv.com/Home/Article.aspx?level

Conversation Starter

The essay lists four areas that require your attention. For our purposes, the five things to consider are probably: 1. your time management, 2. your class attendance, 3. changes in grading and assessment, 4. your responsibilities, and 5. your freedom of choice. Take ten minutes to list for yourself the differences that seem to matter the most to you. Share your list and your thoughts with your classmates.

What kind of textbook is *Huskies Write*?

It's both a rhetoric and a guide. Rhetorics are used in composition class to facilitate learning, meaning there is both information about composition and activities for students to do. There are also handbooks for usage, grammar, and often drills or assignments having to do with craft and style. The emphasis in ***Huskies Write*** is on rhetoric and analysis — the stated purpose of the course. In addition, the text offers a guide to resources available as SCSU. Guides are most often thought of as people who assist others in traveling through unmapped territory. By association, a writer can recognize that a guide, both a book and person, might be needed if the material and skills in a class are either unfamiliar or threatening. It's not that students are entering completely unknown territory since by the time they enter a university or college they have taken writing classes.

However, a guide is often necessary because students more often than not apply what they learned in other classes and sometimes find what they have learned is not a perfect fit to the requirements and demands of the course. Also, writers come to composition from many different situations and different times in their lives. For example, if a student has returned to college after starting a career or family, that student's perspective on a writing community will be different than a student who just graduated from high school. With all their backgrounds and experiences, students need to learn to understand the shared values, expectations, and assignments in the class. They need to *calibrate*.

HUSKIES **WRITE**
A Writer's Guide to Composition and College Life

Rex Veeder · Jason Tham

SKIES **WRITE**
de to Composit

What is calibration?

We calibrate with others when we all have an understanding of our shared purposes, goals, and expectations. This guide is designed to calibrate writers with the requirements, skills, interests, and opportunities of the class. It describes the community of writers and helps those moving into that community feel welcome. Learning writing skills means we understand how to talk about writing, including the techniques, formats, and expectations for writing, and including the process and product of a student's writing. It's good to write about something that interests you and, when necessary, to have the skill of finding something interesting in a topic that is less appealing. This, too, is calibration. Our community is the audience for the writing and also the relationship of the writer to other writers, both present in the classroom and found in publications from books to blogs.

The writing and research community that is important to academic life has a process of getting involved and saying what we believe and know about a topic. Calibration also means learning the shared habits and processes of getting involved and saying something about our topics. In the Philosophy of Literary Form, Kenneth Burke uses an analogy to describe the process of doing research and writing in the context of a party:

> Imagine that you enter a parlor. You come late. When you arrive, others have long preceded you, and they are engaged in a heated discussion, a discussion too heated for them to pause and tell you exactly what it is about. In fact, the discussion had already begun long before any of them got there, so that no one present is qualified to retrace for you all the steps that had gone before. You listen for a while, until you decide that you have caught the tenor of the argument; then you put in your oar. Someone answers; you answer him; another comes to your defense, another aligns himself against you, to either the embarrassment or gratification of your opponent, depending upon the quality of your ally's assistance. However, the discussion is interminable. The hour grows late; you must depart. And you do depart, with the discussion still vigorously in progress. (110-11)

Burke's observation about the parlor is a place to start understanding the community of scholars that students in composition join.

What are my rights and responsibilities?

Writers in a higher education composition class are introduced to, and practice, collaboration, teamwork, and group work. While our mass culture emphasizes competition, it also emphasizes the need for including others. A dramatic way to say this is: "All writing in a college composition class is collaborative." What that may mean to a writer or writers is up to them to decide together, but in doing research and writing we would be hard pressed to find an example of something written in total isolation. Therefore, it is important to consider the responsibilities of a writer and student in a composition class — or for that matter in any class. What follows is the product of Dr. Veeder's classes, collective effort to define those responsibilities. These statements are a good place to start your own discussion of the responsibilities and expectations for behavior and attitude in a class.

Student responsibilities

We are responsible to those who offer us the opportunity to learn and better ourselves. Given this, we believe the following to be core responsibilities to our communities and families as well as to ourselves:

- To take charge of our education by planning carefully and learning how to learn
- To get the most from our investment in time and money contributed by our families, society, and ourselves and to follow through by finishing classes and doing everything within our power to graduate
- To be intentional in contributing to our peers' successes in class and as colleagues
- To learn to be whole physically, mentally, spiritually, and socially
- To use the resources available for our success including supplemental learning opportunities and the social activities available through Student Life and Development
- To be productive in our classes and in the community by applying what we learn as well as learning from our applications
- To understand what it is to be ethical and to act ethically
- To be respectful of each other, new ideas, and other cultures
- To be deliberate in giving back to our communities — our home communities and our University community

Student rights or privileges

Students in Dr. Veeder's classes also collaborated to list student rights or privileges. The distinction between a right and a privilege is always an important one to make, and students considered that distinction in compiling the list. For example, the idea that you have a right "to do what you want" in regard to freedom and the choice of majors is also dependent on the responsibilities of working with others and institutional guidelines. Also, notice that getting an A in class is a right they chose not to include. Again, the list provides a starting place for your discussions in class about student responsibilities, privileges, and rights.

Students have the following rights:
- To choose your major
- To learn about different cultures and approaches to life
- To feel safe, mentally and physically, in our community
- To explore vocation and career in relation to our other studies
- To be considered full participating citizens of the university community
- To have access to decision makers regarding our academic and future careers
- To learn how to learn and adapt to a fast changing society and world

THINKING ALOUD

In considering the class rights and responsibilities, read the syllabus and consider what was written about them there.

Conversation Starter

Students deserve some forms of safety and shelter in a class in order to be able to be successful. How do you describe the feeling of safety or having shelter? What does that mean in your class? Being a participating citizen of the University Community has many of the obligations and rights of being a citizen in the United States. One way to think about your rights or privileges in any situation might be to think of three criteria: Participate, Influence, and Respect. How would you translate these three things into your experience as a student at the University?

Isn't First-Year Composition for English Majors?

The key elements of an English class are writing, reading, literacy, critical thinking, analysis, cultural studies, interpretation, media, and socialization. These elements are clearly not just for English majors.

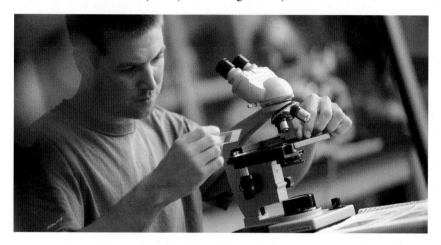

What this composition class means to you and how much you get out of it depends on another old saying: "You get out what you put in." As a cliché, that saying becomes fresh when you consider what English has to do with the rest of your interests. For example, students who are hard wired for English classes usually do well because they are familiar with the culture, the expectations, and the terminology of the discipline of English. They are those students who are comfortable writing research papers. They are used to As and to approval.

Not everyone is hard wired that way. Because people have different learning styles, different backgrounds, and different ideas about who they are, some students think of English class as something designed for and catering to English majors. That's probably true in many ways, in the same way that a biology class might cater to biology students. On the other hand, a biology class may cater to students with interests in science, nature, math, technical writing, or even art. Composition is not only an English class but has much to do with whatever your interests or learning style might be. What students can do to get the most of the class, to put in something that means what they get out is not only useful but exciting, is to see composition as a tool or instrument designed for them as well as English majors.

No matter what your interests or goals, college means you will be writing, reading, and thinking. Composition is a combination of these activities along with ways of getting the most out of them depending on a student's interests and goals.

For example, the National Council for the Teaching of English (NCTE) holds that Twenty-first Century readers and writers should:

- Develop proficiency with the tools of technology.
- Build relationships with others to pose and solve problems collaboratively and cross-culturally.
- Design and share information for global communities to meet a variety of purposes.
- Manage, analyze, and synthesize multiple streams of simultaneous information.
- Create, critique, analyze, and evaluate multimedia texts.
- Attend to the ethical responsibilities required by these complex environments.

Read more: www.ncte.org/positions/statements/21stcentdefinition

The description of needs for an English class matches rather nicely a list of needs for the future compiled by the Institute for the Future and reported in *The Atlantic Monthly* magazine:

According to the Institute for the Future, the top ten skills necessary for personal success and the success of society are:

1. **Sense making:** Ability to determine the deeper meaning or significance of what is being expressed
2. **Social intelligence:** Ability to connect with others in a deep and direct way, to sense and stimulate reactions and desired interactions
3. **Novel & adaptive thinking:** Proficiency at thinking and coming up with solutions and responses beyond that which is rote or rule based
4. **Cross–cultural competency:** Ability to operate in different cultural settings
5. **Computational thinking:** Ability to translate vast amounts of data into abstract concepts and to understand data-based reasoning
6. **New media literacy:** Ability to critically assess and develop content that uses new media forms, and to leverage these media for persuasive communication

7. **Trans-disciplinary:** Literacy in, and ability to understand concepts across multiple disciplines
8. **Design mindset:** Ability to represent and develop tasks and work processes for desired outcome
9. **Cognitive load management:** Ability to discriminate and filter information for importance, and to understand how to maximize cognitive functioning using a variety of tools and techniques
10. **Virtual collaboration:** Ability to work productively, drive engagement, and demonstrate presence as a member of virtual team

Read more: www.challengefuture.org/news/531
See also: "Recalibrating the Classroom: Working and Learning in the 21st Century" **via** http://bit.ly/msxD9U

If you compare the two lists, it is possible that the first list creates the kinds of academic work and experiences that create the skills and habits necessary for the items in the second list. As a student in a composition class, you are working on skills and attitudes that will shape your future and prepare you for your academic career and your life after you graduate. A testimony from a student who just completed a First-Year Composition course follows. Notice how the topics he discusses and what he learned are not just for English majors.

Reflections After Taking a Composition Class: Skills, Career, and Life Goals

Lucas Golliet

In most classes you go to learn specific information, which the professor does not relate to anything but the final test. This class breaks the stereotype. During the course of this class I was introduced to new forms of writing, more effective research techniques, and some interesting concepts. All of these skills and ideas will help me in my pursuit of a job that I enjoy and suits me. Before this class I believed that writing was hard and extremely boring. Throughout this class I have found writing to be quite easy and fun if done in an efficient way. Now I will go into future classes with a lot of writing skills and with a better feeling about writing.

The different styles of writing we used helped me during this class and will continue to help me in the future. We used four major formats for our writing in this class. The "five paragraph form" was the easiest but my least favorite. It was definitely useful to go over since it is the preferred style for many classes at college, especially for in-class writing. This form also allowed us to go over some of the basic writing skills with ease. A research paper is another very useful form to know in college. The research paper covered citing research and putting together what we found as effective sources for the paper. This already helped me prepare the last paper I wrote for another class, and I'm sure it will help me in the next four years of college. Two new structures that were introduced were the recursive journal and the tribal arrangement. The recursive journal was best used for research and finding new ways to look at topics. Recursive journals forced you to look at the idea from different perspectives. As we worked on our journal in class I found that it better rounded out my ideas with how different parts of society view the topic. The most interesting and fun form for me to learn and use was the tribal arrangement. I felt I could better relate to this style, since it dealt with the writer's personal background. While exploring this style of writing I learned about core values and what they mean for me. A core value I have is influence, and with sharing your background you can possibly have more influence.

Researching is the most important part of writing, and I really learned a lot about it in this class. The most useful piece of information I learned about research was if you have a writing block it can be solved with more research. I found this very true in this class and often had to keep going back to the research phase while writing. Through working with the recursive journal I better understood how to conduct research for a paper. It is not strictly the research but the learning about the topic and all views of the topic that provide information. The revolutionary idea I saw with this is interviewing others and finding out how they interpret the topic. Another thing I learned was the correct way to use the research in a research report. I've never really had to write a formal research report so it was a good thing to learn my first year in college. While doing the research and working through the class we used D2L a lot. This was extremely helpful since I am new to using D2L, and it was a great way to learn about the system. Out of all my other classes this was the only one that used D2L, and I am glad we did. Not only was all the information easy to find on the site, but it was a great means of communication which was a valuable tool during this semester. The other site that was helpful to learn about was the Ning site we used for the rights and obligations document. This was a new experience trying to put together a group document strictly online. It proved to be a challenge, but it definitely worked out in the end with a well put together document.

I felt this class was not just about writing and how to write, but I thought it taught some very important concepts. Three of the concepts that provided me the most benefit during this class were core values, strengths, and vocation and career. In this class I found out that my two core values are influence and integrity. These are core values that I already feel like I have been working on for the last four years of my life. With these in my mind I can really focus on what I want to do, but even more it helps me to rule out what I should not do if I want to follow my core values. Having an idea of what my core values are also helps me to focus on the people with which I want to surround myself. Core values are a part of who you are and make a statement about the kind of person you want to become. Strengths were an important part of this class to me because my opinion on what they were totally changed during this class. I used to think strengths were just something you happened to be good at. In fact strengths are what you enjoy doing, and if you practice what you enjoy enough you will become very good at them. Another idea about strengths that changed in my mind was that you had to be a well-rounded person. After looking at the idea closer, it really did make sense that you want a bunch of experts on your team instead of having a group of well-rounded people. Each expert contributes a part to what the whole group is trying to accomplish and together you have a team that covers a lot of ground.

Doing the paper on career and vocation helped me to focus more on what exactly I want to do with my life. It helped me put together a mini plan to get me started during the next five years, and it gave me something to refer back to when I have a question about where I want to go next. The research I did for the topic showed me how to research in a more effective manner since it was the first paper where we used the recursive journal. The research showed me there is a difference between vocation and career, and what I really am looking for is a vocation that I can enjoy doing. These three are what I need to focus on to get where I want to be as I get older.

Writing skills are a large part of this class, and I had the benefit of learning a variety of writing styles throughout the semester and was able to put them to use in the writing assignments. This class also helped to prepare me for the future as I learned more about research and writing research reports, using D2L and creating a group document online. In addition I was given the opportunity to explore concepts like core values, strengths and the difference between vocation and career. This further validated my thoughts on the topic and introduced new concepts that will help me to plan and carry out what I want to do with my career and life goals. Overall I had a great learning experience with writing skills and styles, and was able to learn about concepts that will help me with my short and long-term goals.

Thinking about the text

1. What other questions do you have about the differences and similarities between high school and college?
2. Does it make a difference if you are living on campus or off campus? If so, what difference does it make?
3. What are your expectations for your composition class? What are your expectations for your career at SCSU?
4. Does having a major now make a difference? How does someone without a decided major make the most of the first year and possibly the second year of college?
5. If you could ask one question of the president of the University, what would it be and why?

What to expect in your composition class

What is my role as a student in a composition class?

You can refer to the student expectations earlier in Part One of the Orientation section. However, certain attitudes will help you succeed. One of the major goals and expectations for an academic composition class and classes in general is that you will integrate your ideas with the ideas of others. A couple of analogies might help explain your role.

First, remember analogies are ways of applying prior knowledge to a new situation. When using analogies in composing or when reading them, remember that it is always something like something else... but not exactly. In this case, your role is something like being a quarterback on a football team or being the conductor of a chorus. The comparison between these two roles and your role as a student include the following characteristics:

- There may be a prior plan, but once the game or chorus begins it is up to you to lead, organize, adjust to limitations and circumstances, and perform.
- You must finish the game or chorus.
- You recognize that although you may work hard not everything will be exactly perfect in the game or performance.

Conversation
Starter

The analogies focus on a particular context suggested by one of composition's goals — to integrate your ideas with the ideas of others. Ideas are not the only thing that you integrate when creating or building a composition. There are felt thoughts, for example — ideas that are charged with emotions. Integrating felt thoughts requires social intelligence, and working with them in composition is one way to understand how they change ideas and relationships. List three ideas you have about composition class and discuss or write about how the three ideas are charged with emotion.

- You are in charge of a diverse set of talents, egos, voices, and actions together in one place to do one thing together.
- You may have a coach, a musical administrator, or a composition teacher, but it is your performance, your game, your composition.
- Any quarterback or conductor will tell you that performing or playing the game requires passion, preparation, and performance skill. To be a composer/writer, you will need all three as well.

What do we do in a composition class?

The activities and structure of your class will have common activities with the other composition classes, but depending on the content and structure of class time, your experiences may vary from those of other composition students in other classes. If you are in a learning community, for example, you will be taking more than one class together, and the courses are in some way integrated.

However, all your classes will be focused on composing documents and materials. In other classes, your grade may depend on tests or other forms of assessment, but in a composition class you are mainly assessed on your performance in research and composing. In addition, class participation is important since much of what you will be doing is collaborating with others and doing workshops or studios about your compositions and the compositions of others. A peer review session, for example, is for you and for your peers. If you do not participate not only do you lose out but your classmates do as well. One of the things the writing process and the structure of writing classes will do is help you understand how you depend on each other for learning and writing.

As far as the structure of time in classes is concerned, your experience will depend on the approach of the faculty member regarding the best use of time. Recent work with technology and learning has created a variety of formats for the structure of classes including blended and flip classes. Blended classes are structured with online work and face-to-face meetings. In a class like that, you may spend a class period working in groups and with technology. In a flip class, the faculty member will have you study online materials, often the lecture part of a course, and then come to class to participate in workshops and study groups.

The best thing to do in understanding the structure of the course and the use of course time is to study the syllabus and be in class when the class meets as a whole. Any variations from what you might consider a traditional class structure will be explained there.

I hear people can come to classes if they want to and don't have to attend every class. Is that true?

It is true that your attendance is up to you, but in college the consequences of not attending class are more far reaching than students sometimes understand. For one thing, the English Department's policy for attendance will actually recommend your failure for the course for lack of attendance. The idea is that if you miss enough classes, you will not get the necessary experience to pass the class, let alone do well. Also, composition is an activity course. You do things in the classes that build in a sequence to your final product.

Missing class means you miss out on the sequence. If you have to miss class, make sure to let your faculty member know. It is even a good idea to let those who you might be collaborating with know as well. Finally, if you miss a class, don't decide to not go to the next one or the next because you are behind. That habit leads to failure. It is also a good idea to check with D2L and other communications to see what it is you have missed. It may be impossible to make up the experience, but at least you know what gaps are in your sequence to your final product, be it paper, document, or digital performance.

Here's a do not do: Don't call or e-mail your faculty member and ask if you missed anything important. You did, and asking him or her suggests you think classes are met without anything important going on.

All writing is a social activity. Even the most introverted of people are social and are involved in thinking and listening to others and relating those others to what they are thinking about or composing. If you think you are alone when you compose or write, simply pay attention to what and who enters your thoughts and actions as you compose. Explore this idea by doing a 10-minute timed writing on solitude and how good it is for you. Try not to think of anyone other than yourself as you do — no pets, friends, family, enemies, partners, or attractive possible roommates. Take 5 minutes to talk about your attempt to be alone with your thoughts or write about it and its difficulties.

Answer the following question in a 10-minute timed writing and then take 5 minutes to write or talk about your answer: "Do we want to be alone to write, or do we write to be alone?"

Conversation Starter

What are the basic formats for our assignments?

If you ask this question you recognize that there are formats for academic writing. That is a big step towards success. If you don't ask this question, you should. Your assignment will often be a matter of fitting content, audience, and purpose into one of the basic formats or genre in academic writing or in blending or fusing of them when necessary. Those formats include essays, scientific reports, proposals, analysis papers, arguments, and presentations. You will find these formats discussed in a later chapter of **Huskies Write**. Also, if your class is using another rhetoric, there will be ample explanations of the formats and genre for your papers and presentations.

Here's a discussion and composition starter: Draw a diagram or a picture of two of the academic formats and share your visual with others. Feel free to make your visual model as artful or scientific as you like. Notice this one for the famous five-paragraph theme, a format often used and based on a speech model for writing.

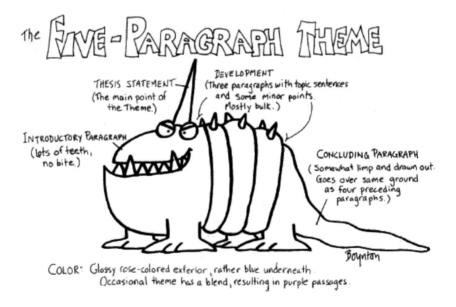

Sandra Boynton's Five-Paragraph Theme illustration. See more: www.proswrite.com

What is the writing process?

Writing process is discussed in detail in a following chapter of ***Huskies Write***. In general however, any sequence of activities that lead to the successful completion of the composition and writing project is a good process. Although there are many writing processes, all of them share common tasks that can be worked on in stages. It is true that all writing processes are recursive, meaning you will find you loop back to each one as you go through any stage of the process. The basic stages most often taught are prewriting, writing, revising, and editing. For our purposes, a stage like prewriting is very hard to define because once you start thinking and working on a project you are actually in the process of writing and composing. Often prewriting simply means the time you invest on research, note taking, and journal writing before you write your first full draft of a paper.

What will my composition faculty be like?

First of all, you should know about your faculty. The term faculty is used through ***Huskies Write*** to identify the director of the class, the teacher, the instructor, the facilitator, the manager, the boss. Your faculty member might be a fully promoted professor at the University, which means she or he is not only tenured and promoted as far as possible but has earned the respect of the academic community for teaching, scholarship, publication, and service to SCSU and the community. In short, the professors are the most experienced and respected in their disciplines and their communities.

You can, if you are deliberate about it, learn from anyone who teaches writing. We all have had faculty at all levels of education that didn't exactly match up with our personality or needs. However, the structure of the institutions and the expectations of the profession mean that you will get someone who knows more about writing and composition, or at least some aspect of it, than you do.

Faculty may be Assistant or Associate Professors, meaning they are working their way through the system to become fully promoted and Tenured. These faculty are, again, highly respected in the discipline, the Department, and community. Your faculty might be a fixed-term faculty member, hired full time by the University but not on a tenure or promotion track. Faculty may be adjuncts who are hired to teach courses but are not tenure-line, meaning they are not hired full time by the University or on a tenure track. Simply, they are qualified teachers, and most often fine ones, who haven't found a permanent position. Finally, your Faculty member could be a Teaching Assistant or Associate. At SCSU our graduate students are in a rigorous program to not only learn about writing and composition but to learn how to teach. You may indeed be lucky to have one of these talented and energetic teachers because they are not only taught how to teach but are supervised by the Composition Director. In all cases, the quality of instruction and the qualities of the teacher are highly regarded.

Second, of course, wondering what your teacher might be like is natural and important. One of the skills is to be able to understand your faculty and to be able to monitor and adjust to their personalities, interests, and approaches to teaching. Be assured, they are trying to do the same thing with you and everyone else in the class. The first few weeks of the semester is often a time of getting to know about each other in these terms. Be conscious and respectful of your faculty and your classmates and take some time to get to know them, how they work and what they expect from you and from themselves as well.

Conversation Starter

Describe the qualities and values you expect in a teacher and in a student. Make a list of your top five expectations and share it with your class in a discussion. Have the class come up with a list of qualities for students and for faculty.

A description of the names and educational background for the Department's full time faculty can be found at www.stcloudstate.edu/english/faculty.asp. Go through the list either on your own or in a group and make notes on which faculty might be helpful to you in your college career and to help you think about your future career(s). What is it they might have to offer you in regard to a future career? Then, study one or two of them and their works by doing some research. Write a one-paragraph biography.

How do I get help if I am having problems with my assignment?

1. Re-read the assignment and support materials for the assignment. Most problems with assignments start with students who do not actually read the assignment and assume they are supposed to do something that is not a part of the assignment.
2. Be specific about what you want to know. In other words, if you can't ask a question about what you want to know, read the assignment until you can.
3. Talk with your student colleagues about what they are doing.
4. Talk with the faculty for the class. There are designated office hours to meet with faculty and many offer specific time in class to answer questions.
5. Make an appointment at the Write Place and talk it over with a tutor.
6. E-mail or ask questions by phone. The need to be specific about your questions is greater here. Without face-to-face contact, it is more difficult to understand what people are trying to explain.
7. Write out your own understanding of the assignment — that is, what would you assign yourself to get what the faculty member wants done completed to your satisfaction and her or his.

What is plagiarism and why all the concerns about it?

The bottom line is that plagiarism is stealing someone else's work — or, cheating by paying someone else to do your work. In either case, the effects of plagiarism are serious and long lasting. Even if someone gets away with plagiarism, he or she has lost out on the benefits of the class. In all cases, the issues of plagiarism are moral, ethical, and legal issues. It is something to be concerned about. It's important that you understand both the letter of the law and the spirit behind it. Mash ups and other fused compositions are not considered plagiarism because they are a form of integrating your ideas with the ideas of others, just like you do in all your academic work. Problems arise, however, when people don't recognize and give credit to the people who did the earlier work. It makes sense to simply acknowledge the work of others and to honor their efforts. For all the professional and legal issues, simple caring for others and showing respect is what you should focus on. Acknowledging others is not a sign of weakness, and anyone who understands what it takes to compose will recognize it is your composition. They will also know you understand that ideas and compositions are always created in a blending of other people's ideas and creations with your own. And, remember, that is one of the primary goals of the course.

Conversation Starter

The original crime of plagiarism in Italy required a trail where the accused had to answer for stealing someone's soul. In this country, plagiarism is often thought of as a crime of stealing someone's intellectual property. Write at least two paragraphs where you discuss the attitudes toward composition and publication packaged into these two definitions.

From Typing to Entering Text: A Literacy Narrative

Adam Smith

As a child, I was very lucky to have a computer at home when most people did not. My dad was going to school for electronics repair, and he was able to get a top-of-the-line IBM XT as a result. This computer cost over $4,000 in 1987, about half the price of an average car. It wasn't obvious to me how special this was when I was five years old, but as an adult it's easy to see the ways in which this early exposure to technology shaped my life.

Of course, it's hard to remember old technology without first being amused by how far things have come! The XT was crammed into a massive all-steel case with a monochrome monitor on top and a keyboard in front. The monitor's purpose was to display things in a lovely orange color, but it also helped keep the air in the room clean by attracting any airborne particles to its screen with static electricity; it consumed enough power to function as a space heater, too. The keyboard's keys clicked loudly enough to be heard several rooms away. It had some primitive games, but I actually spent most of my time on it simply typing words into the command prompt.

This skill soon came in handy. My dad bought a house, and bought an even more powerful computer to go with it — one that could run adventure games. These games had you control your character's movement with the arrow keys, but everything else was accomplished by typing: "open door," "push rock," "get dagger," and so on. I learned a lot of new words and got very good at typing; on the other hand, so many hours of listening to the screechy music probably gave me some kind of brain damage.

I never got tired of games, but the time I spent with them plummeted when we first bought a mouse. It came with a program for drawing, painting, and even animating… and I was completely addicted to it. This addiction got worse when we bought a printer. It was a dot-matrix tractor-feed printer that was as loud as it was slow. It took a long time just to buzz out a single line, but what made it so fun was the paper it used: it printed on continuous sheets of paper joined by perforations. This made it perfect for printing out banners, which would end up all over my bedroom.

Soon after came the most significant upgrade of all: a subscription to America Online. Not quite the same as the Internet at that point, it nevertheless offered an enormous amount of content accessible via phone modem: a technology characterized by frequent busy signals and a cacophonous noise once you finally connected. My interest in computer graphics was fueled through the discussion forums, and I spent countless hours downloading grainy, low-color images of things other people had made. This was very expensive at the time as online services still charged an hourly rate, and my hobby became even more expensive when I spent several months' worth of paper route earnings on a 3D computer graphics software suite. I can still vividly remember all the days I spent in my dad's musty basement hunched over in an uncomfortable, creaky office chair learning every aspect of that program.

At first almost all of AOL's content was exclusive to it, but it began offering access to the Internet as a whole. Back then the World Wide Web was a primitive collection of bare-bones pages, usually black-on-white text with links to other Web pages being bright blue and underlined (or purple, if you'd already visited them). When visiting a new page you took the risk of being bombarded with tacky music and obnoxious graphics. All of this was easy to get past because of the incredible volume of fun, interesting content that was available even then.

The Internet would continue to grow at an exponential rate and through it I would find new friends, hobbies, interests, and knowledge. While computers offer innumerable tools to make our lives easier and more entertaining, it's hard to imagine any single one being more significant than the ubiquitous ability to instantly find information and connect with other people. My early exposure to this important technology was certainly a boon for me, but I can't even imagine how different my life would be had it not existed at all: it has helped lead me down an enjoyable path, and through its influence on me I'm attending school for art as I've hoped to do since I was a child printing out doodles in my dad's basement.

Thinking about the text

1. Marshall McLuhan was one of the first to state that the electronic era was a revolution for humanity, coining terms like Global Village. How do you see yourself and your significant others living in the Global Village the internet has created?
2. Describe what it means to live in the Global Village.

Orienting and literacy: the success kit and a literacy narrative

As a starter for discussion and your literacy narrative, consider the list below. It is a success kit for getting through college (or perhaps life). Do you think the list describes what you have? Can you think of some other things to add to the list? Write a three-page paper responding to the list and write about what you are going to need to succeed and where you might get it. Finally, in one of the paragraphs or more, what part of this list do you think is part of your personal or home culture — the culture you were brought up with?

- A dream for the future
- Family stories
- A relationship with elders
- Friends who understand your highest aspirations
- An awareness of future generations
- An ability to distinguish between what you need and what you want
- Hard work and discipline. (It helps to have done hard physical labor to understand this.)
- A chance to serve others
- Ethical and spiritual teachings to consider and include in your life
- A chance to experience and celebrate the diversity offered in life

Essay Assignment: Composing a literacy narrative

A good way to orient yourself to the class is to consider your past and your dreams or plans for the future in regard to literacy, or the abilities and experiences we associate with being able to read, write, compose, listen carefully, and design. Sometimes faculty and students want to limit the narrative to reading and writing, and that is certainly an option. However, since composition is more than reading and writing texts, it's probably a good idea to consider your literacy as having to do with reading and writing in the Twenty-first Century.

Purpose: To explore and describe your experiences with literacy and to consider what that means to you.

Prompt: Write/compose a literacy narrative in which you describe the story of your past experience with one or more of the literacies: writing, reading, audio, visual design, and presentations.

Format: The essay format is recommended, but other formats may apply. Consider this an autobiography.

Length: Three to five pages. (Remember writing something short requires more work sometimes than writing a long paper. Getting it to the place you like it is more difficult because of the crunch of space.)

Documentation: Use MLA documentation of materials you mention in your autobiography.

Alternative: Pick a fight. Go ahead and make your autobiography an argument for or against some aspect of literacy or some ethical consideration about literacy. If you do the alternative you will need to set the context of your argument by focusing on one experience with reading and writing and then taking a stand, supported by reasons, for or against something.

RESOURCES

You can play a shoestring if you're sincere.

- John Coltrane

You will lead yourself and others throughout your college career and in life. Be engaged. Be aware of resources. Have staying power. Learn by doing and reflection.

A formula for success: Now you = The Captain, the Mission Leader, the CEO.

Orienting to college life at SCSU might seem like a briefing for a mission or the orientation you would get as you start a new position in your career. Because you chose SCSU and college, you have chosen to become a professional, which means you are joining the professions. Being a college student is agreeing to become a leader. The first step in your professional life is to accept that you are your own manager and leader. You will want the resources to gain the interdependence necessary to lead your life.

> We are not nouns, we are verbs. I am not a thing — an actor, a writer — I am a person who does things — I write, I act — and I never know what I'm going to do next. I think you can be imprisoned if you think of yourself as a noun.
>
> - Stephen Fry

Wealth, engagement, independence, and staying power

WEALTH

This chapter is about how and why you should use the wealth of resources and services at St. Cloud State University. You have wealth for engaging with the world of academics in order to gain the skills of independence and interdependence that will foster your success and ability to finish your degree as well as live a good life. You need only go to SCSU's main web page, go to the "Search SCSU" box, and type in what you are looking for to find what you might need, or at least an office or someone who can help you find what you need.

In addition, there are many services that you will use because they are built into your academic life and career from the start including using the Advising Center (www.stcloudstate.edu/advising/default.asp), the Financial Aid Office for applying for loans, scholarships, and grants (www. stcloudstate.edu/financialaid/default.asp), and department advisors and faculty when you are choosing and applying for a major.

In this chapter, we want to explain why you should use the resources and services available to you and offer seven kinds out of the many that are used by First-Year Composition students.

In terms of context for what we suggest, it's good to keep in mind an ancient and contemporary desire and need to find a balance in your life among mind, body, and spirit. If you are deliberate about keeping a balance during your time at SCSU, you will leave healthy, wealthy, and wise. Of course, these three desires for living are relative but you will know what you want and be in a position to either gain all three or improve on the health, wealth, and wisdom you possess when you graduate.

Further, the seven services or resources in this chapter are about useful for being engaged, gaining both independence and interdependence, and having the staying power to do well in classes and graduate.

ENGAGEMENT

Students engaged in their campus and community both academically and socially are found to be more likely to succeed and to stick with classes until graduation. Engagement is blending and fusing your campus life with the lives of others and your communities, both in St. Cloud, Minnesota and with whatever communities you associate yourself.

INDEPENDENCE

We understand the reality and need for dependence. We are in fact dependent on others always because we cannot live alone and because we can't do everything. Moving from a dependence on the world and resources of family or another institution to those at SCSU is sometimes a shock to the system but always in the end good. As they use the resources and services at SCSU, students gain an understanding of being independent and also interdependence. Interdependence is understanding how we work together, how services are tools to get our business done and live our lives. Interdependence is a blend of depending on each other and recognizing we are independent human beings at the same time. It's a good way to live unless you plan on being a hermit forever, and then your chances of not needing someone at some point are slim.

STAYING POWER

Perseverance is a four-syllable word and full of tradition. Learning perseverance and practicing it is necessary for success, since there is no journey, no program, no adventure that doesn't at some point require it as you are getting through to the end. Staying power is a term using three syllables that says basically the same thing. Learning what passion for learning, discipline, and a constant eye on your core values has to do with staying power is probably one of the most important academic and life lessons.

Use SCSU services and resources to increase your wealth, engage your university and community, gain interdependence, and practice the art and discipline of staying power.

1. Academic importance: Active Learning and Integrated Learning Experiences

The fusing of resources, services, and academics is best achieved by practicing Active Learning (AL). AL is a time-honored and proven way to learn something and understand it so that you may apply what you learn. Actually, as Confucius says we most often have to do something to understand.

That doesn't mean that learning by working in the classroom and working with learning tools such as case studies isn't effective. It does mean that perhaps the most effective way to learn something is by practicing it in the company of those you trust and with the assistance of a mentor or facilitator. SCSU resources and services offer an opportunity for service learning and other Integrated Learning Experiences (ILE) situations like clubs, annual conferences, and other community related activities such as the Community Garden.

Read the mission and goals of the community garden and come up with four composition topics that would interest you if you got involved with the garden.

We are a group of St. Cloud State University staff, students, faculty, and St. Cloud community members creating a unified network to envision, plan, plant, tend, and harvest food and flowers together.

The Goals of the Garden:
- To create a beautiful green space for all to enjoy
- To create connection between people and the land
- To educate and expand knowledge about:
  - Sustainable agriculture
  - A variety of cultural foods and flowers
  - Gardening processes
  - Food preparation
  - Natural environments and organic practices
  - Community building
- To share food and ideas
- To provide access to land
- To preserve land, culture, and tradition

Conversation Starter

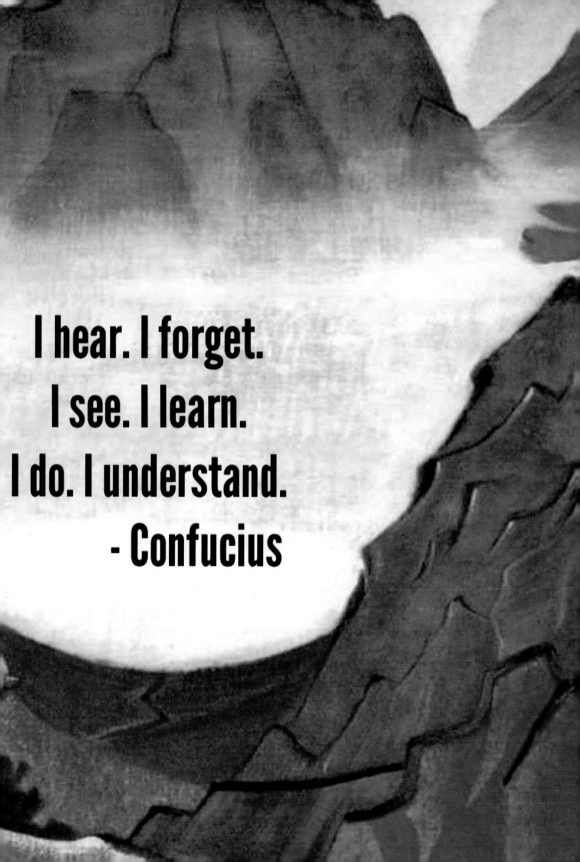

I hear. I forget.
I see. I learn.
I do. I understand.
   - Confucius

The cycle of learning in Active Learning

There is a standard cycle of learning in classes that work with AL:

- Scholarship and reading about a project for knowledge, familiarity, and context for an activity
- Planning the activity with stakeholders in the activity
- Conducting the activity
- Reflecting and evaluating
- Planning for a next step leading from the activity to a goal important to the student and possibly other students and stakeholders

If we consider a medical education, for example, we recognize the familiar pattern of clinical learning. If we consider a civic engagement project, we see how the same pattern applies to working with a community group.

Active Learning and Integrated Learning Experiences are necessary to both academic and personal well-being

Composition classes are intended to help students become a part of the community of scholars and develop the habits that foster success. One of the reasons students don't make it the first year in a university or college is that they simply do not use the support systems and the programs that are put in place to give students the best possible opportunity for achievement. Perhaps as important as good study habits and time management, the skill of becoming involved in the academic community and learning to network and exchange ideas and share work is central to success. If you saw the movie about the creation of Facebook, you may have noticed that it began with an idea that was shared, discussed, and shaped through conversations and meetings. A lunch, coffee or tea, or a meeting under a tree can lead to unexpected involvement and accomplishment. What you study in your classes will stay with you if you find ways to apply what you learned to the needs of others and the conversation of humankind.

Because they are taking liberal arts classes, students study science, writing, literature, philosophy, and society. The idea is to provide an environment where learning is integrated. To increase their opportunities for integration, students benefit from engaging in planned events that offer them an opportunity for shared experiences and personal growth. One event or program helps a students apply what she or he has learned and often leads to another event or program on the same topic until the student creates a network of ideas, opportunities, and career choices through a cycle of learning.

2. ■ Mind, body, spirit

It's important to be aware of, and if possible deliberate about, balancing your life. It is after all something new to you, even if you are starting back to college after dropping out at some point. As you begin the journey of learning and practicing your knowledge in the world - really knowing something — it's a very good idea to pause and make a plan early for your well-being. You can learn to love the constant activity, thinking, and feeling that will shape your life at a college or university.

It's also true that students who don't consider the importance of services before they need them will most likely be confused enough and stressed enough to either not remember what is available to them or simply not

Activity

This list is a summary of websites dedicated to the study of why students fail. Any search will turn up much of the same. Try it. Are there other challenges that are more important to you? I would recommend, especially, the excellent problem/solution approach, "The Best of Times — The Worst of Times," to be found at: www.garfieldgates.hubpages.com/hub/common-problems-for-college-students.

Ten Common Problems Students Face during College:

1. Study
2. Money
3. Job
4. Homesickness
5. Depression
6. Sickness/Health Condition
7. Friends/Roommates
8. Partying
9. Relationships
10. Choosing a Major

It's obvious that any one of the challenges could create a situation where students fail, but often it is a combination of them that drives students to dropping out. Or, students crack under the stress of these problems and really need services and resources in order to be well and whole again.

know where they can get good help. When you are a student at SCSU, these services are part of your wealth. Not using them decreases your chances of success and increases your chances of failing courses or having to quit because of one of the top ten reasons students get into trouble:

Consider the challenges: Top 10 Reasons Students Fail

1. Partying too much and studying too little
2. Being homesick or feeling alone and isolated
3. Being unprepared academically
4. Having financial problems that make continuing impossible
5. Struggling with family issues
6. Having trouble with the academic environment — a lack of familiarity with the expectations and possibilities
7. Not getting mentoring and advising
8. Choosing an area of study that doesn't interest them, usually because they think they have to
9. Working at a job too much
10. Having to move to a different geographic location

Three faculty for ENGL 191 (Amanda Pillatzk, Katelin Moquin, and Erin Schaefer) realized that being thoughtful and deliberate about surviving college and classes is useful and important to their students. Together, they held workshops and took class surveys to find out what First-Year Composition students were thinking and feeling about their well-being. What follows is what they collected. It is useful because if you haven't thought about these things already, it is time that you did. You will notice that there is a long list of things that might help you.

As you go through the list by yourself and with others, pick 10 activities you know you can and will do during the semester for stress and staying sane in First-Year Composition as well as all your courses.

If you think you are going to go to college and maintain perfect physical health, you are wrong. You will get sick. You will get stressed. You will be overtired. The question is not whether this will happen to you; the question is what can you do about it when it does, and what can you do to stay as healthy as possible? Dealing with the health and stress issues that come along with college is a crucial factor in your success every semester. Getting enough sleep, or at least as much as you can, is important.

You are also going to want to learn how to deal with stress. Stress comes from stress factors; for example, these factors might be an upcoming test or a messy breakup. Your stress level depends on how well you deal with these stress factors. When you are not handling stress well, you cannot learn as well as when you are. Your brain just does not want to because it is using its energy on the stress. How you handle stress is really up to you. You might minimize a stress factor by setting deadlines for yourself to avoid getting overwhelmed at the end of a big project. You could also deal with unavoidable stress by going for a walk, getting a massage, or meditating. The best things to do are the ones that work for you. Remember that SCSU also has services for you when issues arrive such as counseling, affordable massages, and health care as well as a pharmacy right on campus!

We asked last year's First-Year Composition students to help us come up with some ways to manage stress, stay sane in ENGL 191, and stay healthy (or deal with it once they were not). The following is what we our ENGL 191 students came up with:

Stress management

- Foster healthy relationships with instructors and classmates
- Don't overwork yourself
- Stay organized
- Take advantage of your advisors and the free counseling services
- Go for walks
- Sleep well
- Eat well
- Safe sex
- Ask for help
- Yoga
- Take a deep breath
- Study during 'quiet hours' or at the library
- Start assignments early to know how long they will take — not all can be crammed into one night
- If you're burned out, take a mental break... it will help in the long run
- Walk your dog
- Gardening
- Fresh air
- Friends that can support you/SCSU Counseling Center
- Doing one task at a time
- Having a schedule and following it
- Write a list of all the things you need to do and put them in the order in which you are going to do them
- Whirlpool
- TV
- Positive mental attitude
- Breathing
- Focusing

- Do as much of the assignment in class the day you get it as you can
- Let everything that is bothering you go no matter what it is
- Pet your cat
- Cat naps
- Hot tea
- Quiet time
- Meditation
- Read a good book
- Driving around
- Window shopping
- Don't cram the night before
- Hot cocoa and do absolutely nothing until you've drank it all
- Rage clean your room (you get so much done so quickly and it leaves you feeling more organized)
- If you get too stressed out, take a break. Don't try to power through
- Don't be afraid to ask for extensions once in a while
- Play video games
- Lawful destruction
- Music
- Bowling
- Listen to country music
- Drive around town with music cranked
- Be yourself
- Take a nap
- Go for a walk
- Sit by the river
- Movies
- Try to smile and laugh as much as possible; still leave time for friends and family
- Helping people work out their problems. It literally helps relieve stress in your body.
- Talking to friends
- Call your mom
- Blast your music
- Stare aimlessly out the window until you realize you stopped thinking about your problems
- Draw (if you like to)
- Nap time
- Don't overbook your days with things that need to be done; relax more
- Stop caring as much; life will work itself out; it always does
- Listen to "Don't Worry, Be Happy"
- Don't procrastinate; try to do presentations and projects first, before everything else
- Try to make life fun; don't take things seriously

What do you find most helpful? What would you add to the list? Share it with your classmates and see what their reactions are.

Staying sane in ENGL 191 (or any class, really)

- Write papers on time
- Allocate time daily to work on papers
- Read the assignments carefully
- Visit the Write Place
- Take everything you can from peer revision
- Come to class every day. You'll lose points and you also miss that lecture if you skip. Copying someone else's notes isn't as effective as having the teacher teach it to you and explain it properly
- Communicate with the instructor
- Participate in class and have a good attitude
- Turn in your work. Some credit is better than none
- Do rough drafts ASAP. You can always revise later, so don't stress about the quality right away. Just get something written as a start.
- Use the OWL at Purdue's website for help with citation
- Study notes
- Study in a group
- Ask for help
- Ask questions
- Use a planner
- Write down deadlines
- Plan for something to go wrong
- Don't procrastinate
- Develop a pattern
- Make more time than needed for obligations
- Schedule a "safety net" time slot for times you fall off the wagon
- Do most demanding things when you are most awake
- Eliminate distractions
- Take study/homework breaks
- Getting projects done as soon as possible

- Prioritize
- Call your mom
- Just sit down and do it
- Moderation
- Motivate yourself
- Coffee gets stuff done
- Take a/multiple breaks
- Set goals; not getting discouraged if you don't reach them. If you don't reach them, make new ones
- Do the easy stuff first — then you feel accomplished and you feel as if you can do more
- Prioritize (partying vs. homework)
- A social life, good grades, sleep; you can pick two, but you can't have all three
- 5-day study plan
- No facebook/twitter/texting
- Daily plan (to-do lists)
- Monthly plan (exams, appt., etc.)
- Plan out what to do each day
- Set times and dates of when to get stuff done
- Don't work too much
- Making lists
- Delete social media apps
- Not putting your papers off until the night before!
- Planning out your papers in advance
- Not being afraid to ask questions and contact your teachers
- Set deadlines for yourself
- If you're writing a large paper, divide it into smaller portions
- Try to do a couple of productive things every day. The more productive you stay, the more you keep up on your homework throughout the day.
- Plan ahead; have a time set aside for each project in advance
- Set goals

Staying as healthy as possible

- Drink lots of water
- Waking up to work with the right mentality
- Don't take long naps — take power naps
- Walk or bike instead of drive
- Drink more water and snack less
- Cook your own meals from scratch
- Take things in moderation (e.g., smoking, drinking, unhealthy foods, etc.)
- Get a workout partner
- Play outside
- Eat fruit
- Sleep!
- Don't overwhelm yourself
- Swim
- Not eating when bored: find something to preoccupy yourself with other than food.
- Take vitamins and eat a balanced diet
- Swimming pool/skating, skiing, etc.
- Walk every day for at least an hour

When things go wrong in your composition class

When things go wrong in a composition class, it is often because of one or more of the 10 Common Problems. It's difficult to write well when you are depressed or physically ill. Poor study habits, one of the most common problems, often caused by a lack of time and task management. Students might occasionally find themselves writing a paper at the last minute. However, if the last-minute-I-work-best-under-pressure experience becomes a habit, the chances of writing well and feeling good about it are greatly reduced. In short, planning writing time and research time is a key to success.

Many students, used to the habits of high school, do far too little research and far too little writing. Most of the advice in this guide is intended to get students reading and writing as much as possible. Next, students may not have had much experience in working together. Group work is not necessarily collaboration. Collaboration is working together to a common end with everyone contributing. When people collaborate, problems with relationships and even problems with roommates can become mirrored in class activity. Also, students do not ask enough questions about specific issues with content and with writing tasks. Rather than asking how they are doing in general, students are better served by asking about how they are doing in a specific area — paragraphing for example.

It is also important to get to know how and when to talk with your writing teacher. Office hours are provided for conference time. A writing conference usually takes from ten to twenty minutes when it is focused on a specific issue. Many writing teachers are willing and able to help you find resources for other problems with studies and life, but they are seldom certified counselors. In other words, what students most often get when they want to discuss something going wrong will be advice on how to deal with class issues and references to resources available through the University.

Seven resources to leverage your college experience

Both your academic services and the services of Student Life and Development (SLD) are included in the following list of seven resources most needed by students during their first-year experience. The core values and mission for SLD are an indication to you of how important it is. Search the website for Student life and Development to recognize the richness and depth of support for students and faculty offered by SLD's staff. Wanda Overland, the Vice President for SLD says in her welcome message to students:

> Because learning is a campus-wide experience, we are committed to providing positive, enriched environments so students can succeed inside and outside of the classroom. By becoming fully engaged in both academic studies and campus life, they gain a greater understanding of themselves, their beliefs, and passions and how they can make a difference in the world. The staff, programs, services, and facilities are available to assist in learning and taking advantage of all that SCSU has to offer.

Mission

The mission of Student Life and Development is to support and serve students by providing the co-curricular opportunities, programs, services and environment they need to develop personally, socially, and professionally.

Student Life and Development Outcomes

We seek to assist students to:

- Be globally-aware and support diversity
- Be self-aware and strive for meaningful relationships
- Be an engaged member of their various communities
- Take full advantage of opportunities for learning
- Explore leadership
- Live a balanced and purposeful life

Read more: www.stcloudstate.edu/sld/default.asp

The outcome goals for SLD resonate with the goals of your First-Year Composition class and the resources and services in this chapter. The following seven categories of resources and services are ones the students at SCSU have found particularly useful during the first two years of their academic career and beyond. Sometimes important or even critical services and resources are not used or not used enough because students don't realize they are provided for them. If you will invest some of your class and study time to these services and make some note of how they are useful and important for you, you will be prepared when you need them. You will need all these services at some point during your academic career.

1. Go to and use the Write Place

The Write Place is the English Department's writing center and provides excellent tutoring and group assistance for composition students, from First-Year Composition to Masters students writing their theses. It is the place to start if you need any help at all with your writing that is not easily available from your faculty or your classmates. Many faculty in First-Year Composition will recommend the Write Place, and ***Huskies Write*** certainly recommends it for its expertise, kind and thoughtful tutoring, and its offering of skills for study and doing well in your academic career. Dr. Carol Mohrbacher, the Write Place Director, offers this introduction:

> Dear First-Year Composition Students,
>
> The Write Place has been a valuable and free resource for SCSU writers, since in 1968. We work with all kinds of writers from all fields, not just English. We work with you at any stage of your writing assignment from brainstorming ideas to polishing the final draft.
>
> We also conduct workshops every two weeks on a variety of writing topics. See the Write Place website for the schedule. Because we have been in existence for so long, we also have hundreds of handouts on a range of writing issues from punctuation problems to how to write and organize specific types of papers like the rhetorical analysis or the research paper.
>
> Sincerely,
> Dr. Carol Mohrbacher, Write Place Director

Where is the Writing Center?

We have two locations. The main writing center can be found in Building 51, in Room 117. The library location is located in the library in the James Miller Learning Resources Center building on the first floor in Room 127B.

Do I need an appointment before I come to the Writing Center?

Very often, consultants are available for drop-in appointments. However, just before and during midterm and in the weeks leading up to finals week, we get very busy. If you want to ensure that a consultant will be available to work with you, please make an appointment ahead of time.

How do I make an appointment?

You can make an appointment by going to our website at www.stcloudstate. edu/writeplace and then by clicking on "make an appointment with a consultant." Or, if you prefer you may call 308-2031 and our receptionist will help you make an appointment. See our website for our open hours.

The Write Place's website consists of its operation hours and a form to schedule an appointment with tutors.

When in the writing process should I make an appointment with a consultant?

Generally speaking, the earlier in the process you begin to work with a consultant, the more help she or he can give you. We encourage you to come in when you are in the planning and early drafting stages and to continue to work with a consultant throughout your writing process. Most students who use our services come in when they are nearly finished with a writing project. We are certainly willing and able to help at this stage, but we know that there are limits to the depth and quality of feedback we can provide when writers have limited time for revision.

What should I bring with me to my Writing Center appointment?

If you are working on an academic assignment, bring your syllabus and any written description of your writing assignment your professor may have given you. Bring a draft of your paper, pens and pencils, a notepad, and any research notes you are working from.

What should I expect during a Writing Center tutorial?

You should expect to do a lot of talking and thinking. Whether you are planning your writing, drafting and revision, or are working on final editing, your consultant will be asking you lots of questions and giving you plenty of opportunity to ask your own questions. Consultants won't tell you what to write, nor will they copyedit papers for you. Instead, they will help you learn to think like a writer — particularly, a writer in an academic community. They will model the kinds of questions academic writers ask themselves. The consultants will help you think about who your audience is and how to write in ways that your audience will recognize as being legitimate, convincing, and compelling. When you are talking with your consultant about citations, syntax, or copyediting issues, they will teach you the concept and then give you opportunities to apply the concept with their help. You'll recognize this as "learning by doing." Writing Center tutorials are highly interactive.

How many appointments can I have with a consultant?

We recommend you make no more than one tutorial a day. Tutorials are labor intensive for both writers and consultants; you will lose your ability to concentrate and to remember your conversation after an hour. Also, because of high demand for our services, we ask that you not schedule more than three hours of tutorial time each week. We want to cultivate independence and confidence among student-writers at St. Cloud State University. Becoming too dependent on our consultants will be counter-productive. For additional policy guidelines concerning length and number of tutorial hours per week, call 308-2031.

What if I am unable to come to the Writing Center due to distance, illness, or other inconvenience?

Although we recommend a face-to-face consultation as the most effective working arrangement, sometimes it may be difficult to come to the writing center. In that case, you may want to try making an online appointment with a consultant. These appointments are synchronous; that is, they are done in real time via a chat function. Both the writer and the consultant are able to see and work on the paper, which is uploaded to our online module. For more information, contact us at 308-2031.

> Tear out sheets at the end of **Huskies Write** include six of the most common information sheets students request from the Write Place: Comma Rules, Effective Thesis Statements, Rhetorical Analysis, and Suggested Structure of an Argument.

2. Go to and use the James Miller Learning Resources Center (Miller Center)

The Miller Center will become a second home for you during your academic career. The sooner you understand why students say "It's Miller Time," the sooner you will start to feel at home in the scholarly world. Many of your First-Year Composition faculty will organize tours of the Miller Center and an introduction to the fine services and resources available to your scholarly research and composing. There is little at SCSU that is more directly important to faculty and students alike.

Here's an introduction from Dr. Cindy Gruwell:

Academic Resources, Academic Success, and Learning Resources

Cindy Gruwell

Who are the Jumping Frenchmen of Maine? What role did Minnesota play in the Dred Scott decision? How do independents affect presidential elections? Unless you know the answers to all of these questions, you would have to seek out information to understand and provide the answers. Unlike your formative years in high school, college and universities require you to dig deeper than what is easily available through Wikipedia, YouTube, and similar resources. Though often informative, they can lack the integrity and vetting needed to support writing and research. So what resources should you use? How do you know if a book or journal is considered scholarly? Where do you find information about citation styles used in papers, speeches, or projects? Look no further, the library located in the Miller Center can provide the answers and assistance you need.

As you progress through the process of research you will find that you are building upon your subject knowledge while obtaining information needed to support your academic work. What's at stake? The integrity of your work and the ability to prove to yourself, instructors, and peers that you have explored your topic and are comfortable enough to present your thoughts, analysis, and conclusions as needed in your coursework. The amount of time you invest in your research will shine through in your final project.

So where do you start? Many courses, especially ENGL 191 and CMST 192, set aside time to visit the library and take part in a variety of general orientation activities. But it shouldn't stop there. Library instruction sessions are meant to familiarize you with our resources and provide pointers for navigating our web page, the gateway to an abundance of materials available in print and online. As you move along in your academic career, you will be challenged to perform research with a varying degree of depth and quantity of resources. By utilizing the library's web page to search for books, scholarly/popular journals and newspapers, government documents, DVDs and other materials, you will can maximize the results of your research with supporting documentation. Keep in mind that getting started is not always as easy as it seems, but remember we are here to assist you.

Of course you may explore the library's web page on your own (lrts.stcloudstate.edu/library/default.asp). Take advantage of the Library Search tabs located in the middle of the page or the Subject Guides below, which provide dictionaries, encyclopedias, journal databases, and websites focused on a particular area of study which ranges from art to chemistry. In addition, you may use the Research Project Calculator (stcloud.lib.mnscu.edu/rpc) to guide you through the research process from start to finish. But, if you really want to maximize your experience, stop by the reference desk and we'll point you in the right direction with real-time answers to questions and personalized consultations! Not able to stop by, you also have the option of calling us at 320-308-4755 (Toll-free 877-856-9786) during reference hours noted on the library's web page, dropping us an e-mail at askref@stcloudstate.edu, or by speaking directly to an academic librarian through the AskMN chat service available through our Ask A Librarian page (lrts.stcloudstate.edu/library/research/askalibrarian.asp). The point is you have options and should never hesitate to ask us for assistance. We are here to serve you and are committed to helping you achieve academic success!

Conversation Starter

The role of the library has changed dramatically in the last ten years from being a place where books were stored and offered to being an information center that includes the best possible technological resources for scholarly work. Go check out a book, find a scholarly article about its subject matter, and talk with classmates about what you discovered by going on an adventure of discovery.

THINKING ALOUD

Getting information off the internet is like taking a drink from a fire hydrant.

– Mitchell Kapor

3. Take advantage of the services provided by Help Desk and Information Technology Services

If there is one thing we can depend on it is that we will have to use a computer and access information from the internet. If there is a second thing we can depend on, it's that we can depend on our forms of digital communications to develop a glitch or the intrusion of a hacker, or even a meltdown of all our work at the worst possible time.

Being wise and reasonable about the wide array and great wealth of software and hardware available to us is important. It is harder and harder to get an education without digital resources, and perhaps it is almost impossible. There are those who hold out and go with analog for almost everything, but even organizing a meeting with them or sending them papers or materials is very difficult. For better or worse, we are living in an age of bits and must learn to succeed in the digital world. With that in mind, SCSU's Help Desk and Information Technology Services are essential and — students and faculty have found — approachable and thoughtful about our needs as technology users.

Becoming familiar with and using SCSU technology services is probably one of the first things students enrolling at SCSU. Your HuskyNet ID and all the services that come with it would be, a very few years ago, almost an embarrassment of riches — Web Space, Desire2Learn (D2L), university email, and all the e-services available will ensure you are a citizen of the Twenty-first Century if you use them and become familiar with how to use them well. Your SCSU Help Desk will be the place to start when one of the glitches appears on your computer, or tablet, or phone.

Conversation Starter

Take a tour of the e-services at SCSU by accessing huskynet.stcloudstate.edu. Notice the resources available and make a list of the resources you will be using the most and that you will want to study up on. Make sure to include D2L since it is most likely a part of your First-Year Composition class and many if not all the rest of your classes.

4. Integrate diversity into your academics and your life

In the Survey of Student Satisfaction a few years back students said that they had learned a lot about diversity at the University. White students also said that they had not actually met or had a relationship with a person of color while at the university. What appears to be ambiguous is actually an indication of how information is not useful unless put into practice.

SCSU is dedicated to providing an environment where all students can thrive. If you come from a rural area, it is possible you have not had a sustained relationship with a person of color. (This demographic is changing since more people of color are indeed living in rural areas.) Students will have opportunities for developing a sustained relationship, which simply means a relationship that means something to them, during their years at a university or college, and people of color will have opportunities to meet people who are from a different demographic from them, a different country, or a different religion. Of course color is not the only description that indicates difference and worldviews; family background, physical abilities, and sexual preference are other indications of difference. The important thing about difference is that we need others and their difference to grow and learn and thrive. Sometimes difference threatens our view of the world and even, depending on circumstance, our ideas and beliefs about who we are and our families. Learning to thrive with a conscious engagement with difference is one of the most exciting and challenging experiences at SCSU.

SCSU has a reputation for enrolling students from all over the world. The English Department's Intensive English Center (IEC) and its English as a Second Language program (ESL) are internationally recognized as being of high quality. ESL students are one example of how difference improves our lives and our education because opportunities to share with a perspective of world views are all around us at SCSU. What follows is a message about ESL students from one of our staff and faculty, Julie Condon.

THINKING ALOUD

St. Cloud State is honored for its commitment to diversity and inclusion in the December issue of Insight Into Diversity magazine. The University is among 48 recipients of the Higher Education Excellence in Diversity Award (HEED), which recognizes efforts to include diversity such as gender, race, ethnicity, veterans, people with disabilities, and members of the LGBT community. (www.stcloudstate.edu/news/newsrelease)

Native and Non-Native Speakers of English Learn Together in ENGL 191

Julie Condon, College ESL Coordinator

ENGL 191 is a wonderful conglomeration of students in which everyone comes together for a common purpose: to establish a common set of expectations and required skills for academic writing at the university. Students come to us from all high schools of Minnesota, other states, and the world. Some come as transfer students with some experience at another institution. Others come to us in a process of continued education after some time in the workforce, the military, or in raising a family. I wish to focus on those students who come to us from a background in which they largely used, and learned in, a language other than English.

In our English Department, we have College English as a Second Language (ESL) and Intensive English Center (IEC) students. ESL students take one or two semesters of writing in preparation to join their peers in ENGL 191. IEC students study English language full time for several semesters to reach a suitable level of academic proficiency. "ESL" as a term has largely gone out of use. More recent terms are English Language Learners (ELL) or English for Academic Purposes (EAP).

When students have finished ESL and moved to ENGL 191, how can we refer to them? I think we can say "non-native speakers of English." That would make those students who have used English as their primary language and means of learning "native speakers." We will find that non-native speakers (NNS) will come to ENGL 191 with a huge variety of life experiences. Some of them may have graduated from Minnesota high schools. Some may have come as immigrant adults with their previous education in another country and another language. Some may have college degrees already in another language. Others may have just graduated from high school in distant country and another language and have just arrived in St. Cloud a week before classes began.

As native and non-native speakers and writers of English embark on the journey of ENGL 191, they can benefit from several pieces of advice to make working together more comfortable.

Group discussion is a common style of shared learning in the US; however, it may not be common in some other countries. Thus, it is valuable for all members of a classroom group to consider what makes good group work. First, every member must participate. Introduce yourself to your group members and learn their names. If you don't hear the name clearly or know how to pronounce it, ask the classmate to repeat it more slowly and try to say it. Next, give every member a chance to speak. In American English and academic culture, we typically leave less time for someone to respond or jump into a conversation. If you are working with a non-native speaker, give the speaker more time to respond. If the student has not participated, ask him or her directly for their input, and then wait until he or she has finished speaking before going on. Third, if you don't understand what someone said, DO ask them to repeat it. That is not rude. It is ruder to go on and ignore what was said. Class members need to learn to negotiate meaning and become accustomed to the way that others speak English. Not only students but also professors come from all around the world to SCSU, so this will be a necessary skill to develop.

Peer review is also commonly used in writing classes in the US, while students with previous education outside this system may not have been asked to review others' work. The instructor may have been seen as the only person qualified to make any assessment on a student's work. In an ENGL 191 class, if you are asked to review your classmate's draft, you can expect to have been given a rubric or questionnaire through which to analyze specific aspects of the work to which you are assigned. In this way, classmates have a responsibility to each other to be current with the material presented for the class and to learn together through such exchanges.

As new college writers, native and non-native speakers will have a variety of strengths and challenges from individual to individual. The first point I like to make to my students is that just because someone has graduated from American high school, that does not automatically make him or her a good example of a student. We are a public university which accepts a huge variety of students. Our system might be characterized as "easy in, hard out." Students are given the chance to succeed in college, but admission does not guarantee success. Nationally and at SCSU, 72% of students who begin college in the fall of their first year will return the next year. That means that 28% won't be back the next year, for various reasons. Some of your classmates will be well prepared for college, and others will not. When we think of factors for success in ENGL 191, much of it has nothing to do with language: the ability to get up in the morning and get to class on time, good time management to complete all assignments and preparation for class, family responsibilities, financial management and the need to work many hours to pay for school or not, the ability to manage class resources such as handouts, school e-mail, and D2L use, and many more. These are personal skills that make a good student regardless of English language ability. Thus, while Abdi may be building his English vocabulary and makes grammar mistakes, Hunter hasn't read the day's assignment before class and hasn't checked D2L in 5 days. While Brittany can whip out a three page essay in the last hour before class but did not go back to check her punctuation, Junko has been considering methods of complex sentence combination and has revised her thesis statement over several days.

In conclusion, don't assume that "Americans" will do better in ENGL 191 just because they are native speakers. Don't assume that the immigrant or international student next to you doesn't understand the class because she never speaks up in discussions. Get to know each person individually and discover his or her strengths to a good class member and build your learning community.

Student Life and Development offers resources and help in negotiating difference. Students also learn about difference and the forces that shape our understanding of the world in classes, clubs, social events, and informal gatherings. Students also need to remember that they are "different" to someone. Writing, studying, and talking about how we are different and how we identify with those who we feel uncomfortable around and those who make us feel comfortable will be one of the main topics in a college or university. The lessons learned and the relationships created in working with this topic and with difference can make a student's life better and his or her career better as well.

Diversity will be one of the main areas of content and discussion in your First-Year Composition course and in many other courses. One place to start finding information and activities that will inform you and help you in feeling at home at SCSU is through the SLD Student Services site: www. stcloudstate.edu/campuslife/student-services.aspx

Conversation Starter

We are often much more diverse than we think we are. Someone might be a person of color, a Republican, and have family that immigrated to the United States only a few years ago. We all have an investment in personal and community engagement with diversity. Take five minutes to make a list of all the different kinds of family, community, and interest groups that are a part of your life. Then, make a list of how they represent diversity in your own life.

All ESL (English as Second Language) Students Welcome!

Douglas LeBlanc

*F*eeling a little anxious about taking ENGL 191? Maybe a little intimidated? That's okay! After all, you're taking an "English" class intended for native speakers of English. In fact, you may have heard some of your native English speaking friends talk about dreading this class themselves. However, even though ENGL 191 is a challenging course, it is a fantastic opportunity for all students, no matter their language background, to improve their abilities in writing and analytical reading. These skills are some of the most important assets for a college student. After all, there is plenty of reading and writing waiting for you in your future classes! What better chance to improve those abilities than through a course designed to do just that. Below is some advice and some thoughts to help ESL students succeed in ENGL 191.

Your Instructor
ENGL 191 is a challenging course. Don't try to navigate on your own! To begin with, try to establish a relationship with your instructor. He or she will be guiding you the most in your quest to become a better writer. Share with your instructor your background experience with the English language and your concerns about your abilities. This will help your instructor help you the most. And be sure to regularly check your e-mail and D2L; many teachers communicate with their students via these tools. Communication is really important to succeed at an American university!

Your Fellow Classmates
Don't be afraid to establish relationships with the native English speakers in your class. Remember that even American students are often nervous about taking a writing class. So don't feel intimidated! You have a unique perspective to bring to a writing class!

The 5-paragraph-theme
Be prepared to think outside the 5-paragraph theme. It is true that this essay format is commonly used to teach American writing styles, and you may have taken writing assessments in which you were supposed to use this model. However, ENGL 191 will ask you to take

what you have learned from the 5-paragraph theme and expand your "thought boxes," if you will. Don't be afraid! Experiment! We all learn by doing and re-doing.

Grammar and Punctuation
Are you worried about your abilities in grammar and punctuation? While these are important, know that native speakers of English often struggle with grammar and punctuation too! So you're definitely not alone. Keep working at this, and always take the time to do your best. And don't forget to visit the Write Place to help improve these skills (see page 67 to learn more about the Write Place).

Thinking about the text

ESL students do sometimes have a harder time in an English speaking and writing class. If you are a student from outside the immediate area of SCSU, you will share the feeling, perhaps, of being dislocated and sometimes homesick. Being homesick is one of the experiences new students in any institution share when they are "not from around here." Try the following as 1) a way of imaginatively participating in the lives of ESL students and 2) a consideration of the advice in terms of how it applies to you as an ESL student or as a "domestic" student:

1. Do a 20-minute timed writing in which you describe your experience starting at SCSU and beginning your FYC class. ESL students describe the experiences "as if" you were someone from around here and domestic students describe the experience "as if" you were from another country. As an extra for domestic students, in some part of your writing compare the area to the area you are imagining coming from. Share your writings with a group and talk about what you felt as you wrote it, as you share it with others, and what the experience of imagining means to you.
2. Read the letter at least twice and highlight or underline what you think applies to you. Then, make a list of the elements of the advice that you would consider useful and helpful for your FYC class. Next, talk over your lists with your classmates to see what elements on the list relate to your own experience.

5. Attend conferences, join clubs, and connect to the wider community — including service learning

Civic engagement

SCSU is recognized as a campus encouraging and supporting a mission of civic engagement. The importance of this is that the University deliberately creates, encourages, and supports programs, curriculum, and resources that promotes your engagement with communities important to you. One of the features of our involvement is service learning.

Service learning is a credit-bearing educational experience in which students participate in an organized service activity that meets identified community needs and reflect on the service activity in such a way as to gain further understanding of course content, a broader appreciation of the discipline, and an enhanced sense of civic responsibility. (Robert Bringle and Julie Hatcher, Office of Service Learning, Indiana University-Purdue University Indianapolis)

Our Department of Campus Involvement is the center of our civic engagement programs and projects.

Mission

The Department of Campus Involvement's Civic Engagement Program is St. Cloud State University's community service center. Our mission is to provide students the opportunity to develop leadership skills, a sense

of belonging, and civic responsibility through involvement in meaningful service. We strive to promote reciprocal service that benefits both the individual and the community.

The Civic Engagement Program:

- Helps organize volunteer opportunities
- Serves as a clearinghouse of service information
- Works to promote academic service learning
- Strives to build strong relations between SCSU and the larger St. Cloud communities

Read more: www.stcloudstate.edu/campusinvolvement/volunteer

Student clubs and organizations

In the practice of active learning, civic engagement is a core piece for you and for the University. Also, becoming involved in student clubs offers an opportunity to meet like-minded people who are interested in making a difference and making the world a better place. The best resource for finding the club you might be interested in is www.stcloudstate.edu/campuslife/get-involved/default.aspx. Note both the number and depth of the organizations available to you in these quotes from the website:

"Thanks to nearly 250 clubs and organizations, there's always something exciting to do. Hit the river with the SCSU Crew or catch some air with the Skydiving Club."

"Check out Greek life by pledging a fraternity or sorority. Learn about other cultures through an international student organization. Take a Spring Break service trip to Montana. The Department of Campus Involvement can help you do all those things — and much more."

"Have an idea for a fun event or an interesting speaker? Contact the University Program Board (UPB). Student-run UPB offers a variety of activities and entertainment, including speakers, trips, films, events, exhibits and performances."

"Fitness, aquatics, intramurals and outdoor opportunities are available through Campus Recreation. Students can use an array of outstanding facilities, including a climbing wall, pool, field house, Husky Stadium -- the Mississippi River — and more."

Conferences and special events

SCSU has several exciting conferences offered each year. Conferences and special events are opportunities for both service learning and campus engagement. Many internships, service learning opportunities, and class projects are a part of the events and conferences. Here are just a few of the conferences and events that you may attend and even volunteer to work with. You will through the processes of Active Learning, find your attendance and engagement a core part of your education rather than what has been called "academic enrichment." You will find announcements and information of University events at www.stcloudstate.edu/events. Here are four examples of the kinds of conferences and events found at your University.

Student Research Colloquium

St. Cloud State University's annual campus-wide Student Research Colloquium (SRC) promotes research, scholarship, and creative work in collaboration with faculty as a vital component of higher education. Faculty, graduate students, and undergraduate students from St. Cloud State University and regional universities are encouraged to participate. Industry sponsors are also invited to attend.

The goal of the SRC is to bring together students, faculty and members of the community involved in scholarly and artistic activities representing a range of disciplines, including creative arts, mathematics, business, social science, humanities, physical and life sciences, and engineering. (www.stcloudstate.edu/src).

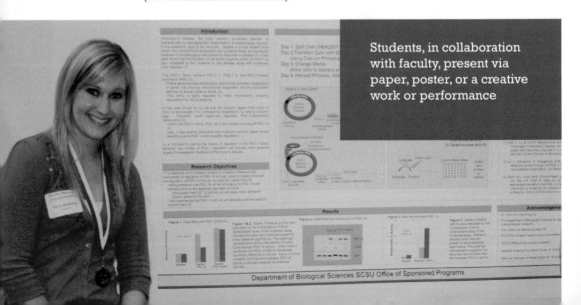

Students, in collaboration with faculty, present via paper, poster, or a creative work or performance

Power in Diversity Conference

The Power in Diversity Conference will offer opportunities for personal growth and leadership development to college students through a variety of workshops, keynote addresses, and programs. The conference theme "We are the Change: Where do we go from here?" will set the stage for keynote speakers and workshop presenters to identify ways that participants can lead the way in promoting positive change in our society and our world, moving past mere tolerance and ultimately resulting in affirmation of all people. (www.stcloudstate.edu/mss/powerindiversity)

"I know there is strength in the differences between us. I know there is comfort, where we overlap."

- Ani DiFranco

Conversation Starter

Do 20 minutes of research about one of the conferences in this section. Take 10 minutes to brainstorm on how the conference might fit into your topics for classes or for your career interests. Share your thoughts with members of your class.

Survive and Thrive Conference and Festival for the Medical Humanities

We are dedicated to improving the odds of survival and living well through education. We are committed to engendering and facilitating restorative therapies for the sick and injured, their caretakers, families, and medical professionals. We welcome all who are dedicated to saving lives and the aesthetic experience in healing regardless of the kind of illness or injury. (www.survivethrive.net)

We have to do something together to make empathy work, and we either have to be explaining something — revealing a discovery always in the making — or inducing others to cooperate with us in some way – perhaps only to validate our experiences and thoughts. In one way or another, narrative medicine and medical humanities are involved in these things, and when we participate together in the motives for a community of spirit, mind, and act, we can say it is therapeutic and also a work of art because one of the basic human acts (some argue instinctual acts) is to do art in the company of others, especially in the company of those we trust. (www.survivethrive.net/blog)

Winter Institute

The Winter Institute is an annual summit hosted by the Department of Economics, School of Public Affairs, St. Cloud State University. Minnesota is famous for its winter season and every year we use this opportunity to gather the best minds in the region and the country to share their thoughts and ideas on various economics issues with audience from Minnesota and the Midwest. The Winter Institute is an important forum for the members of the community to generate ideas that can foster growth and development in the greater St. Cloud area, central Minnesota, and beyond.

Many prominent economists and policy makers, for example, Alfred Nobel Memorial Prize Laureate Milton Friedman and Federal Reserve Chairman Benjamin Bernanke, have been our keynote speakers at the Winter Institute in the past 49 years. Visit our Past Winter Institutes for more information on previous speakers. (www.stcloudstate.edu/winterinstitute)

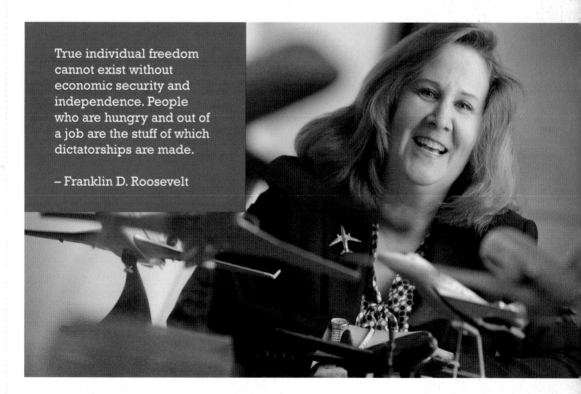

True individual freedom cannot exist without economic security and independence. People who are hungry and out of a job are the stuff of which dictatorships are made.

– Franklin D. Roosevelt

6. Know how to practice health and well-being — including counseling center

In the orientation chapter, we described the importance of balancing mind, body, and spirit. It's important to know the resources available to you to maintain that balance or to find help when you need it. Your composition faculty will often ask you why you are missing class, for example, but they are not in a position to be a physician or a nurse or a counselor. It's good to know who those people are on campus. In addition, there are clubs for working out, a great student gym, and other resources for health, both physical and mental.

The balance necessary in regard to spirit is important to all students, and your choice of how you maintain spirit in the mix is clearly up to you in a public institution. In considering how to maintain the spirit, religious institutions may not be what you choose. If you do, there are clubs and other resources available to you. If you choose another way, you will find resources for the maintenance of the spirit, such as yoga or meditation. Your mind will be something that the environment and mission of SCSU will nurture and challenge. In regard to physical health, it's wise to develop a program for yourself that includes exercise, nutrition, and sleep.

SCSU also offers services for help and workshops in both physical and mental health:

Health Promotions Department

The Health Promotions Department is probably the place to look first for information and resources. The Health Promotions Department is dedicated to get the facts out to SCSU students about a variety of different health topics (signs, posters, presentation, booths, newsletters, awareness weeks, one on one, etc.). Also feel free to drop in and join the Condom Club, pick up a variety of different brochures, ask questions about various health issues/concerns (we might be able to help you with resources), and inquire about volunteering and internships as well as about assistance for presentations and programs. You will see us around campus at various events in Atwood and Garvey and a variety of classrooms and residence halls. Can't find what you are looking for? Stop by (Health Services at Hill Hall) or send us an e-mail at: hlthpro@stcloudstate.edu. If you would like us to do a presentation for your group or class on Sexual Health, Condom

Bingo, Nutrition 101, Stress Reduction, General Health or other health topics please contact: tsshafer@stcloudstate.edu. (www.stcloudstate.edu/healthservices)

Counseling and Psychological Services

Counseling and Psychological Services (CAPS) is a department within the Division of Student Life and Development that helps undergraduate and graduate students cope more effectively with personal, mental health, and academic issues that arise in their lives.

We offer free and confidential personal counseling and consultation to promote personal development and psychological well-being and assist students in defining and meeting personal, academic, and career objectives. (www.stcloudstate.edu/counseling)

7. Participate in the Common Reading Program

New first-year students received a copy of the selected text during your Advising and Registration Days session, giving you the opportunity to read the book by the start of your first semester at St. Cloud State. The purpose of this program is to provide a common academic experience for all new first-year students, which integrates both curricular and co-curricular activities throughout the year. In addition to events around the book at your New Student Orientation in August, many of you will use the book in at least one class you take during your first year, and all of you will have the opportunity to participate in a wide variety of programs throughout 2013-2014 related to the book and issues it raises.

Your participation in the common reading program will:
- introduce you to the nature of collegiate academic life.
- cultivate a sense of community with your new home at SCSU.
- help you develop connections with faculty and staff and other students at the university.
- get you involved in campus activities with related programs and events.
- enrich your classroom experience with an shared intellectual experience that cuts across courses and co-curricular opportunities.

Read more: www.stcloudstate.edu/commonread

Conversation Starter

What is this year's common read? Your FYC class may be working with the book and the many resources for research and discussion available through the Common Reading Program. If so, how will the class be working with the book? Take a look at the materials at the web site and discuss what you find. For example go to www. stcloudstate.edu/commonread/beyond.

Assignment: Do not despair — plan and implement instead

Considering the challenges in the 10 ten reasons for failure, the student list, and the following information, write a 4- or 5-page proposal and/or prepare a presentation that allows you, and perhaps others in your class, to meet the challenge. As you do, consider the services and resources in the chapter. Remember in a proposal, you will want to define the problem, discuss the specific context for your own proposal for solving the problem, and give a plan that you intend to implement during the semester.

- Natioanlly, 50% of college students have a job. SCSU's rate is higher. Do some online research to find out how much higher. Where did you find this information?
- 20 hours a week at a job may actually contribute to your success as a student. Over 20 hours a week and you will most likely suffer consequences.
- Balancing home responsibilities, job responsibilities, and class or school responsibilities is important to your success.
- Nontraditional students who have a family, a job, and are seeking higher education are especially in need of a time management plan that works for them. Remember that the estimated time necessary for study is about three hours a

week outside of class.

- In a recent survey, SCSU ENGL 191 students reported studying 10 hours a week for all their courses.
- Needed time for class work = around 20 hours a week. Actual time reported = 10 hours a week.
- What are some strategies for finding quality time for study?

WRITING PROCESS

3

It is good to have an end to journey toward,
but it is the journey that matters in the end.

- Ursula K. Le Guin

The process for composition is proof that all writing and composing are social. You may need to be alone, but your thoughts and composing always involve others. Get used to it because you are making the world together.

You're on an adventure - like moving, a road trip, or wrestling a bear.

Different people at different times see the journey or the end as most important. In composition, your journey is the process of getting to the end of the document or presentation. Focusing on both the process and your product at the right times is focusing on time management and composing skills that will help you thrive. The process is indeed a trip, a journey, an adventure.

> And what, you ask, does writing teach us? First and foremost, it reminds us that we are alive and that it is a gift and a privilege, not a right.
>
> - Ray Bradbury

Questions and answers about the writing process

What is the purpose of a composition process?

The composition process is a way for you to be a scholar. Being a scholar means having a willingness to explore a topic in terms of a specific context in relationship to a personal interest in order to add knowledge that will be interesting and useful to an audience. Commit this to memory and practice being a scholar by engaging in the composition process.

How do I become a scholar?

There's a commonly known story about advice for retail business that says there are three things to remember — location, location, location. If you want to understand what it means to work analytically and rhetorically, to be a scholar, remember the three things important to success in academic and, thus, scholarly composition — context, context, context.

When someone asks a scholar what is the truth, the scholar will answer, "It depends." What this doesn't mean is that the scholar doesn't believe in truth. What it does suggest is that scholars understand that scholarly work requires us to think in terms of what something means in relation to the specific context of the question. This is a scholarly core value.

It you are to act in a scholarly way, you want to make sure you have settled for yourself what the context for your research and composition is as well as the context of your assignment. Figuring out the context is part scholarly and part personal.

For example: You have an assignment that asks you to investigate something that both you and your peers are interested in. The scholarly part of the assignment begins with the idea of investigation — which suggests among other things the exploration, invention, discovery, and research associated with a topic. The personal part is choosing that is important to you, and you believe is important to the class.

How can I be personal and be academic?

Let's try an example. There's a long-standing piece of advice to novice writers that they should write what they know about. In an academic course, you will more likely work with 10% to 20% of what you know and the other 90% or 80% will be about something you need to know about and that interests you enough to want to know more about it and then tell someone what you have found out.

For example, you were probably asked to write about what you did during summer vacation at some point. Let's say one memorable experience during the summer was going to a music festival and that you were excited about the bands playing Rhythm and Blues. In your First-Year Composition class the experience of the music festival becomes a work site for composing, using a process that is recognized as scholarly by the academic community. You might, for example, start with a description of

THINKING ALOUD

How you think aloud is sometimes a matter of you simply insisting on a specific topic that relates to the general class topic. However, if you want to be systematic about it, make a list of your interests on one half of a piece of paper and a list of topics associated with the class on another. If you study the lists for a moment, you can draw lines between those things that match up. Any one match is enough to get you started bringing together personal interests and class topics.

the festival and describe some of the music. You might come up with a phrase or an idea that inspires you – such as, "The blues are the rock upon which roll was founded." You might do research on musical history and race relations, and wonder why Black African Americans sometimes object to white people singing the blues. You might then use music and history to highlight an issue in race relations or explain why the blues help heal the divisions caused by race and color in our country. Your personal experience, plus meeting the requirements of the assignment and some investigation, discovery, invention, and research has added to the knowledge we share as a community of scholars. This is another way to think of the composition process.

Conversation Starter

Take any interest of hobby, career, family, relationships, or curiosity with science or the arts and trace a personal interest to an academic topic. Next, share it with a group to see if together you find similar topics of interest and academic concern. Consider how you are practicing in a community of scholars.

Is there a standard composition process?

A standard description for a composition process is the following:

1. Prewriting
2. Drafting
3. Revision
4. Editing
5. Proofing
6. Submission/performance/dissemination
7. Evaluation and assessment

THINKING ALOUD

There are two commandments to keep in mind as a composer in any community, be it scholarly or not. Consider them a contract you signed when you started composing:

1. Thou shalt not bore the audience or waste their time.
2. Thou shalt not confuse them without good reason.

Remember, there's a recognized process but it depends on how you use it. All writing requires reflection where you monitor and adjust what you have done with what you did before and what might come next. Taking time to do this is one of the important elements of a composition process — think of it as a period of adjustment.

The truth is that a composing process is always messier than described and is always dependent for depth and accuracy on recursiveness. Compositions benefit from the composer recognizing the need to be deliberate about being recursive.

Being recursive is stopping to contemplate what it is you just did and how it affects the other things you did before and what you might do next. There are many terms for this; the most popular right now is metacognition, or the practice of being aware of your thinking. The word is heavy with implications but in practice it means to pause, consider, look for patterns of connecting ideas, words, associations, or data, and then adjust what you need to in your composition.

Almost everything in the process requires us to monitor and adjust for effects to the other states or stages described. There are no clear-cut stages, but there are times when you should concentrate on one task in order to give it the attention required to finish the project and finish it well.

There are, therefore, times when you will focus more on one of the tasks associated with composition than at other times. Since you don't have all the time in the world, you will want to deliberately integrate the recursive act into your composition process.

THINKING ALOUD

There are times to research and times to design, times to plan and times to draft, times to revise and times to finish revising, there are times for dissemination and times for the evaluation of successes and short comings, times for listening to others and times to shut out other voices, times to review with peers and times to judge peers' critiques, times to take notes and times to resist note taking. There are also times to be confused and worried and times to be so sure of what you are doing that it makes your head hurt and feels good at the same time.

Can you put what you just wrote another way?

Always — the great thing about the writing process is that often we have to come at the same information from a different perspective. It's another period of adjustment. Another way to look at the composing process is that it is a natural process that we practice all the time. Again, the complexity of language adds a thrill and an animation of ideas and words to the project, but that is half the fun.

There are two analogies that are popular for describing the composing process: growing and building.

What I like about analogies to the writing process is that they take what seems to be a really heady and fuzzy set of activities and makes them more physical and, therefore, better known and understood. I am convinced that the writing process is no different from all the other processes you have mastered during your life, or at least practiced. We can acknowledge that because language is involved, the dynamics of composition are complex and sometimes mysterious to us. Still, the processes for making or growing something help explain what we do when we want to get something done.

I will confess that the idea of an animation of ideas and words seems awfully airheaded, but it is something that can be tested in your practice. What follows in terms of an explanation of the writing process might help a bit. One of the pleasures of scholarship and university life is being air headed about ideas and words. You will get to do that, and you will also get to try to explain what your airheaded thoughts and theories apply to the context of the moment.

Editor's Note

Remember, we are peeking behind the curtains to see how tricks of the trade work. Finishing a composition project is making a mess and then cleaning it up. Writing and composing, like building or growing anything, is messy. All of our efforts at making the process and stages of composing clean and neat are actually fictions created so we can get something done. The trick in to the composing process is to believe the fiction of a progression by stages long enough to get the work done. Besides, once you see the benefits of the process, it no longer will matter whether it is a trick because you will want to trick yourself over and over.

Re-read Kenneth Burke's Parlor (page 15) for a combination of a composition process and joining a conversation. You are joining a conversation of scholars.

Editor's Note

We like to imagine the composition process as growing something if we consider the naturalness of the process and if we have a slightly more artistic approach to composition. The feeling of growing a report is really a good feeling. But, growing one takes about as much time as it takes to grow tomatoes. Also, growing your composition suggests a rather romantic notion of waiting for inspiration or writing your paper while sitting in a warm bath with a glass of wine. All this may be good or bad, but it is likely that under the constraints and time pressures of academic courses growing a composition is more a matter of luck than inspiration. It has the same effect on results as "I work best under pressure," which is one of the ideas that come from a romantic view of composition – that is that *expression* comes from compression. If you want a diamond, you have to put it under pressure, but if it isn't an industrial diamond you have to wait longer than a semester to get results.

I like to grow my books, essays, poems, stories, reports, and proposals. I am aware that doing that takes a lot of time that I may or may not have. If there is a deadline, and any writing for someone has a deadline, I can't wait to put down roots that I might not already have.

So, the best academic analogy for the writing process (please try others for yourself if they help) is building something. We build to a blueprint on ground we prepare. We gather materials to build, and there is a systematic way to build something. You can start at the top of a house, for example, but I promise it will lead to more complications. To build something, you have to have a schedule and you have to depend on others at some point in the process to help you build things you know little about. To consider a composition as a worksite and your approach to be a builder is to make things a lot easier for everyone involved.

So, consider the writing process as directions for building something and let something grow — perhaps a lawn — if you have time.

An example of a scholarly process and composing:

The writer and Chicano, Jimmy Santiago Baca visited SCSU and in a writing workshop described how he wrote one of his books of memoirs. He explained that he started with the plans to build his house in the New Mexico mountains around Sante Fe and how he wrote about building each room to write the book. What happened in the kitchens he grew up in? How does that influence how he is building his kitchen? Baca used his home

building as a way of organizing his memories.

Research: There are a lot of reasons to do research on a project like Baca's, and you can see how it is personal and also relates to a more general audience that might be interested. For example, what was going on in history during the memories available to Jimmy that add a historical perspective to the memories and the house he is building? What materials that go into the house have something to do with his memories — rocks, wood, earlier and later manufacturing techniques? Would it add to the memoir to discuss measurements and why the kitchen is big or little? Is there an architecture and building process associated with mountain homes? What does this home have in common without what makes it different from a home in the suburbs, farm country, or city?

Format: The genre of composition needs to be fitted to the expectations of an audience. Thus, the decision about how to structure the project has to be an early one. For example, a memoir is a good thing to write in an English class and might work in others under certain circumstances. However, if you are writing for a scientific audience with a specific assignment, you will want to adjust according to scale and approach. The discussion of the house might be a part of your introduction and a viewpoint from an engineering point of view might be your report.

Conversation Starter

How might a psychologist, a geologist, an archeologist, a sociologist, and a geologist contribute to Baca's book? How does this example help you understand the community of scholars?

What happens in the composing process?

For each project compare what you are doing with the process. If you are leaving something out, be able to explain why.

1. **Prewriting:** The exploration, invention, discovery, and research associated with a topic, and planning a strategy for finishing the project.
2. **Drafting:** Getting a version of your project in analog or digital so that you have something concrete to work with — the sooner the better.
3. **Revision:** An adjustment to the draft made after evaluation and assessment to the project thus far. A period of adjustment. A rhetorical analysis of the work. Revision usually involves a restructuring of the projects documents or presentation(s).
4. **Editing:** Work with style, sentences, and paragraphs for clarity and effect.
5. **Proofreading:** Turning the presentation, document, and whatever is associated with the writing project into something without disruptive surface errors. Often a separate part of the process from editing.
6. **Submission/performance/dissemination:** Doing a presentation, handing in a document form or publishing the results of the project either online or in analog.
7. **Evaluation and assessment:** A final review of the project by you and by someone responsible for assessing your successes and shortcomings. (We all have both.) This usually sounds and feels like a grade. One way or another, it is. A grade is simply a measurement of the assessment according to the blueprint for the assignment.

Conversation Starter

How you combine personal and scholarly interests is sometimes a matter of you simply insisting on a specific topic that relates to the general class topic. However, if you want to be systematic about it, make a list of your interests on one half of a piece of paper and a list of topics associated with the class on another. If you study the lists for a moment, you can draw lines between those things that match up. Any one match is enough to get you started bringing together personal interests and class topics.

INVENTION, DISCOVERY, AND RESEARCH

Discovery consists in seeing what everyone else has seen and thinking what no one else has thought.

- Albert Szent-Gyorgy
Nobel Prize Winner for Medicine

The joy and thrill of Invention, Discovery, and Research (IDR) is an invitation to a life of learning. The journey to your destination begins with exploration, moves to knowing where and why to find information, and ends with a vision (a design) for making something only you can make.

You're an explorer, going where someone went before to discover it with your vision.

Consider what Chuck Palahniuk says in *Invisible Monsters*: "Our real discoveries come from chaos, from going to the place that looks wrong and stupid and foolish." Consider what Bill Stafford says: "A writer is not so much someone who has something to say as he is someone who has found a process that will bring about new things he would not have thought of if he had not started to say them." Invent. Discover. Research.

> Writing is like breathing; it's possible to learn to do it well, but the point is to do it no matter what.
>
> - Julia Cameron

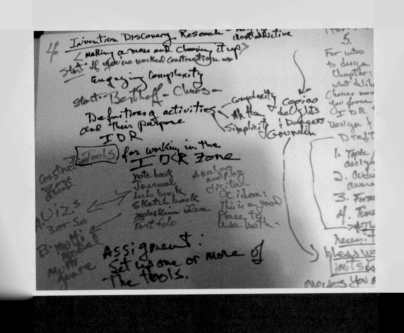

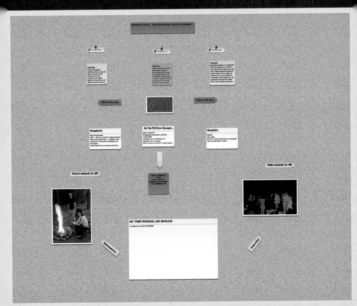

Organizing the Chapter:

Design after Invention, Discovery, and Research

Invention

Increase knowledge, identify patterns, generate topics, be creative, have some fun, ask questions, answer questions from others and those you want to ask your questions to

Discovery

A place between invention and research where a person delibrately makes notes about patterns, ah-ha moments, and questions of how to follow the leads provided in the invention process to do more systematic research

Research

Increase knowledge, be systematic (find this because it is related to that and I want to know why and how), follow sequential agenda (a scholar needs to have a plan for research), focus on specfic sets of questions, work linearly (or use progression or sequence rather than random association)

Move this way

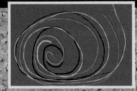

Move this way

Complexity

Look and look again.

Copia — there is a world of related material

Immersion and emersion — jumping in and coming out of the pool of knowledge and information

Seeing things from many perspectives

Ah-Ha/Pattern Recognition

Eureka, I found it!

Recognizing connections, patterns, relationships

Sometimes you're looking for it

Sometimes it's a surprise

Best to create a written or visual sequence

Simplicity

Balance

Clear Space

The five-to-seven rule (what you remember)

Focus on main point(s)

Private moments for IDR

Private moments for IDR

This is a discovery board. Ah ha! There is a sequence and an order in the complexity!

Get Your Personal Life Involved

To compose is to be in the world!

Contemplation

Celebration

IDR: Passion, preparation, performance, pondering

Recently, the Dean of The Schools of Health and Human Services, Dean Monica Devers, talked about a speech given by The Minnesota Lynx Coach Cherl Reeve in which Coach Reeve said the keys to winning at the game of basketball are passion, preparation, and performance. I know the coach would agree that we can add pondering to the three since to contemplate, assess, and analyze your performance and preparation is a key to having a passion for the game and for winning. In your game of composing, the same elements are central to your success as a scholar and composer.

The practice of the skills, arts, and sciences of Invention, Discovery, and Research is the way to move from simply summarizing other people's knowledge to adding your own to the human project of increasing knowledge and wisdom. Whether you knew it or not, when you enrolled at SCSU you signed on to being a professional and to the project of creating knowledge. The degree you seek is a certification that you are a person who believes in that dedication and the project of making knowledge. It is not the key to a job, but it is the key to a profession. Whatever you do after graduation, you will be a member of the profession you chose to practice with passion, preparation, and performance.

Conversation Starter

Take ten minutes to jot down the things in life that you would like to add knowledge about. Then, in a group discuss your jottings or list. Finally make a class list of what those topics and themes are and keep them for reference when you feel like you don't have anything to write about.

One way, then, to describe what your role in a composition class is that you are a knowledge maker. In order to do that, it is not enough to read something and write a summary and leave it at that. You will be adding your interpretation, your point of view, your application of what you read, found out in an experiment, or discovered while researching a collection of artifacts, or a bone chip, a report on sustainability of grass lands, a work of art... clearly the list could go on as long as there are projects and assignments that interest you or you are required to do.

To make knowledge you need to practice the arts and sciences of Invention, Discovery and Research. The practice of these three things, IDR, is one of the most important practices to take up in your academic career and in your life after graduation.

An overview of the purpose of IDR

Many times while research helps to answer a question, invention and discovery helps someone ask questions that allow for a more sequential research process. Like Research, Invention and Discovery activities may include activities such observations, interviews, and surveys, but the activities are more exploratory in nature and usually less structured than research-driven activities. Invention and Discovery seek to generate ideas and questions, explore associations, discover patterns, and chart out sequences, relationships, and topics or themes of interest to the writer in relation to a topic of interest or an assigned topic.

IDR: Making a joyful mess and finishing with a clean well-lit, space

It may not be what you would expect to hear in a composition class since we want at some point to produce something that is clear, understandable, and meaningful to the audience. The problem is that to have meaning to the audience it has to first have meaning for you, and meaning isn't something you borrow from anyone — you have to make it yourself. The phases of IDR are ways of discovering knowledge and meaning from it.

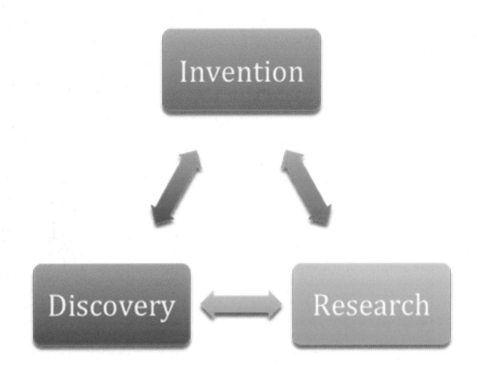

THINKING ALOUD

It's popular to attribute the imagination to muses and magic. Society seems to praise the imaginative person and fear her or him at the same time, perhaps out of fear of the real power of imaginative thinking to change the world. In terms of FYC, it's a fact that we should recognize the very natural and human gift to be imaginative and sharpen our skills in order to be deliberate in its practice and practiced in its use.

Invention: A hectic gathering of information for the purpose of exploration and adventure

Invention is an artistic, scientific, and rhetorical practice of gathering as much information in one place as possible. Since invention is actually addictive, it's a good idea to limit the time in any given project. On the other hand, you will want to invest enough in invention to hit upon what it is that you have a passion for. Thus, in respect to passion, preparation, and performance, invention is the domain of passion. You can even spell it with all caps if invention works: PASSION. In fact, one way to move from invention to discovery and back again is to work with a sketchbook, notebook, or journal during an invention phase to identify for future reference what really interests you with the word *passion*. If you do, it will help you trace patterns of interests (systems of interest) that then become the associated topics for your discovery and research phases. As with all composing activities, you may not be able to imagine this sort of thing actually happening to you unless you have done it already or until you do it. Remember that to understand you have to do it.

In order for invention to work, you need to make things strange, pack information with no seeming relationship into a small enough space for those bits of information to resonate with each other - for the strange to become familiar by association.

THINKING ALOUD

Invention is inviting chaos into your life by doing mind experiments. Chaos, to the scientist suggests not disorder but a complexity. In working with invention and discovery, it is important to play by the rule that whatever you gather has something to do with everything else you are gathering. If you say or think something utterly mad, you have to be able to say to yourself and others that there's truthfulness in what I just thought or said, and now I am going to explain why. In the process of invention leading to discoveries, however, it would be a waste of time to spend too much time explaining.

For example, the topic assigned or agreed upon by you and your faculty member in a class with a naturalist or medical emphasis could be about animals, plants, or trees — biology if you like. Your invention phase would involve collecting as much information as possible and making notes and annotations about that information. It is important to use both analog and digital information and to collect it in some way that allows you to have in one place pictures, quotes, recordings, data, and any other bits of information that suggest to you it has something to do with your topic.

Getting your mind experiments started is a matter of bringing a lot of information together and then looking at it from as many perspectives as possible as in asking questions like "How is a tree a bird?" Or, "What if this paper clip were a universe?" But, playing the game *requires* you to explain why a bird is a tree and why a paper clip is a universe. A hint in many situations is to consider any comparison from either the micro or macro perspective – at what level can we say with honesty that we know that a rock lives. Or, we can consider the same question from a matter of context: Under what conditions might we say a rock lives? When we do this, we are generating knowledge. As we work out the chain of ideas associated with a living rock, we make discoveries and are surprised by things we have not thought before.

> A good response to a question of "What do you want?" would be "Something I haven't thought of yet."
>
> **Editor's Note**

Once you have your data set (why not call it that) you can then play with it both physically and mentally by pairing up even outrageous images and texts to see what invented thoughts come from them. If you are a scientist, you might call this pure science in terms of doing an experiment just to see what happens. If you are an artist you will recognize it as something you might do when you want to encourage inspiration. Make something and look at it again and again. Make something else and see what happens in your head. In fact, this is a creative act whether science or art, a shared site of serious playfulness.

Discovery: Eureka, I have found it!

(A cry of discovery of displaced water and suggestive of a response from an idea you have when an apple hits you on the head while you are napping under the tree.)

Discovery, is the "Ah-Ha" experience of discovering new knowledge and the mapping of patterns you recognize as important in helping others understand your new knowledge generated during your mind experiments we named invention.

It's a good idea to be aware of when you shift from your mind experiments to an attempt to understand the pattern of relationships you see emerging from them. You will want to discover a pattern of ideas, images, notions, arguments, and or other associations among the bits of information. Once you do, you are being an explorer, discovering new territory.

Like invention, discovery is best practiced in journals, notebooks, and sketchbooks using either analog or digital tools. In many cases since your invention phase asks you use a multimodal approach (sound, images, visuals, and text) as well as a multi-genred one (podcasts, texts, books, quotes, pictures, poems, literary nonfiction, and fiction), you will be using both. The thing you should do during the discovery phase is be able to physically connect the dots, so to speak, among the information bits that attract you or seem to you to be related.

Discovery is gaining a perspective and thinking methodically about it.

Whereas the invention phase asks you to invite chaos and complexity into your world, the discovery phase will be an experiment in beginning to explain why things are related for you, why what you are passionate about deserves your attention for the preparation of your project's performance or publication. What that means is you will make a number of attempts at times before things begin to make sense. And, you know you have discovered something when your seemingly random and disassociated information suddenly, it seems, makes sense because of some point of view or perspective that brings elements of the invention together as a reasonable explanation of what was once so strange and jumbled.

THINKING ALOUD

In discovery, you identify patterns, relationships, and sequences that are only evident when you discover them among the jumble of information gathered during your invention phase. The process by which you explain the connections among your areas of interest is thinking methodically, that is with a design in mind. You are, in facts beginning to design your presentation or document. When you read this, you will probably find your head hurting. When you invent and then begin to contemplate your inventions, it will be understood.

THINKING ALOUD

Invention requires a hectic gathering of information from a variety of sources and genres. Invention and discovery often use a journal approach to gathering and responding to information from a wide variety of sources. The activities of invention and discovery are most associated with imagination, creative thinking, and a holistic perspective. You are more likely to get the whole picture.

> **Conversation Starter**
>
> Take your list of what you want to contribute knowledge to and make one or two things on the list strange by comparing it to something that seems outrageous — such as gene therapy and football. Explain under what circumstances the comparison is truthful. Again, be social and share your mind experiment with someone.

Where the invention and mind experiment phase asks you to suspend disbelief in a strange association, the discovery phase asks you to practice a process of asking what things look like and how they relate after you have tried a point of view that joins them. For example, using our "a rock is alive" experiment earlier, the perspective that allows us to recognize how it is truthful or how a rock and life are related, or the pattern leading us to an understanding of how they were related would be most likely at the subatomic level. All things resonate and vibrate, even if they appear to us to be solid and still. The same, of course, is true of this book or the place you are living in. It might be somewhat unsettling to realize everything is vibrating, but it not only makes sense but also can be truthfully explained. Recognizing the connections and charting them in some way is an act of discovery.

Identify patterns and generate topics

One good way to move from your mind experiments into the discovery phase is to ask questions about what you have invented:

- Who would want to know about this?
- What is it that I have just found out exactly and what might it have to do with my topic?
- What's the elevator speech (an abstract) that summarizes what I have created here?
- If I were to doodle or draw a picture of these ideas, what would it be?
- What are the things I want to find more about?
- If I were to advocate for something after doing these experiments, what would it be?

Another pattern identification starter is to use an aphorism as a prompt to begin to write about your mind experiments. An aphorism is a saying or some quote that allows you a perspective to jumpstart a timed writing or for writing at all. When used to generate writing/composing, an aphorism is a prompt.

Conversation Starter

Do a 10- to 15-minute timed writing prompted by the following quote and then be social and share your mind experiment: "The creation of something new is not accomplished by the intellect but by the play instinct acting from inner necessity. The creative mind plays with the objects it loves." - Carl Jung

You may want to look through the notes on your mind experiments and write *interesting* or *passion* next to places that seem to have caused you to write, draw, or scrawl the most. By sheer volume you can notice what sparked your interest and can identify what you want to know more about.

In order to move from the discovery phase to your formal research phase, you need to move toward simplicity and clarity. Whereas the invention phase invited complexity, you are now *imposing order on some part of it*. In order to do so, you have to practice the strategies often suggested in the prewriting phase of the composition process — Outlining, mind maps, flow charts, the use of apps for an electronic tablet if you have one, lists of things that you then can clump together under the heading of interesting stuff, and finally a review of these things and a list of what is most important to you in the categories created and lists generated.

By the time you do this, you will have found something that requires you to do more research and is connected to the assignment or topic of interest. It is during this phase that you create a research plan with your topic at the head and your topics of interest for research under it.

Conversation Starter

Write the topic for your assignment on the top of a sheet of paper and then list research questions generated from your invention phase. When you have done this, you are ready to begin formal research.

Formal Research

Formal research is a way of answering questions and finding new questions to ask. Primarily, its purpose is to find materials related to a specific pattern of information. Thus, it is often sequential and planned in advance. It is the best known of the methods for gathering the right kind of information for a pattern, relationship, or sequence that is already identified. Research is most often the activity associated with sequential and linear thinking. Research is often associated with a notebook and is most often associated with finding high quality — and sometimes a wide variety of — sources. Research can also refer to experiments and forms of information gathering such as surveys, interviews, and polls. Research is seeking to solve a problem, answer a question, or find the best way of doing something. Formal research most often relates to a specific issue.

Re-read the essay by Cindy Gruwell in Chapter 2 and then with your lists of interests and research question set up a research calendar that includes your main research questions, your strategy for researching those questions that includes electronic and at least one on site visit, and a schedule of writing your paper or preparing your presentation that is coordinated with your research plan.

Editor's Note

Formal research is the kind of research recognized by all academic disciplines as the foundation for your compositions. When you do formal research, you are working with established systems of research that have been tested for generations. If you want to answer a question, you go to Information Services and the library at SCSU, either physically, which we highly recommend, or electronically. More than likely during your FYC class you will and should do both. Many faculty will assign time in the library and hold classes there. Information specialists and educators are an important part of your adventure in learning — your entrance into the world of creating knowledge. Faculty from your FYC classes and faculty in the Learning Resource Center have a partnership in facilitating your research. Work with all of them and your peers to establish a plan for research and then carrying that plan out.

Assignment

Here's an example of inventing and discovering acting together and working with a context that allows you to generate ideas for writing and research:

Overheard in a conversation: "I saw your eye twitch and heard a sigh. I know you care, but do you care about me?"

1. Context:
A. Two lovers sitting together.

B. A patient and a doctor in an examination room.

Starter questions for contemplation: Does gender make a difference? Does the look on their faces make a difference to you?

2. Perspectives:
A. The lovers just had an argument.
B. The patient and doctor are discussing a diagnosis.

3. Consider and make notes:
Consider the overheard conversation first from one lover's perspective and then the other. Consider the conversation first from the patient's point of view and then from the doctor's. Notice how it matters which person in the conversation is speaking.

4. Shift again:
Add a third person — for the lovers, someone who is in love with one or both of them and for the doctor and patient, a nurse or family member. Again, notice how the relationship of the third person to the other two changes what the conversation might mean.

5. Move towards research:
Make a list of questions about what you and others have been talking about. You may find yourself focusing on medical protocols or the dynamics of triangulated relationships. You may want to know more about the kinds of illnesses or injuries you imagined the diagnosis to involve. You will find, whatever the questions, that you have discovered topics or invented issues that are in fact very real and could involve a more organized process of research. For example: "What are the signs of a failing relationship?" Or, "What difficulties arise with intimacy between a patient and physician?" Once you have generated a question or two, it is easy to consider a list of related questions that you can then use in your research agenda as well.

For discussion and composition:
Notice how invention and discovery are creative activities in that you are asked to imagine the scene of the conversation and a possible backstory. Forms of creative invention and discovery actually lead to papers, fiction, video, and other compositions. For example, if you were to read a poem and interpret it you would be starting a literary analysis. If you read together and did an analysis with classmates of an editorial, you could be easily establishing the context of an argument or persuasive essay. However, in each case, because First-Year Composition is a research, composing, and analysis class, you would want to consider what deliberate research would contribute to your composition. Thus, invention and discovery will help you recognize an audience and format for your writing as well as topics, themes, and questions.

DESIGN AND DRAFTING

Often the hands will solve a mystery that the intellect has struggled with in vain.

- Carl Jung

At this point you have answered a question that drives the IDR experience: "If I believe this to be true, what difference does it make to the way I think and what we must do together?" Your audience needs you to make your case for your insights, your discoveries, and your vision of what we must do. Design a plan for this and create a draft (prototype).

Detective, reveal the mystery.

All good readers of mysteries know the climax of a mystery is a revelation of not only who is guilty but also why the detective discovered the guilty party or parties. The classic scene is a gathering of suspects in a room with the detective declaring he or she has solved the case, and we all feel the suspense and tension as everyone waits for the revelation. Design and drafting is the process of how you will reveal the information in your case. In doing so, you will design a sequence of information that leads to your conclusions and then create a draft, prototype, or document.

> You know my method. It is founded upon the observation of trifles.
>
> - Arthur Conan Doyle, *The Boscombe Valley Mystery*

Design and Drafting: Clean up that mess!

Both the comic book ranting of the editor and the exclamation point at the end of the header for this segment are *hot* appeals. A *hot* appeal is one that is intended to be obvious. Both the comic and the exclamation point are also reminders of the urgency involved in composing during a class and the importance of reflective thinking. (1) You have a schedule to meet. (2) In order to understand composition you must do it. (3) You don't want to take unreasoned action or do something that you think is worthless.

In the last chapter IDR was framed in motivational terms: passion, preparation, performance, and pondering. Of the four, pondering seems to be the least motivational, but it is what starts you along the road to doing a design and drafting your paper or presentation. The critical part of invention is inviting chaos in, which creates your motivation and interest (passion). The critical part of discovery is pattern recognition, and the critical part of formal research is being systematic; you want to move from A to B to C in order to cover what you have determined to be the important research questions, and in both D and R, you are preparing for something. The performance, then, begins with designing and drafting your project paper/presentation.

As a final part of the context of this chapter, remember that you did IDR with the assignment in mind. Designing and drafting are also the next step in the phases (or parts) of the composing process. What follows are the best advice and activities we have right now for being successful.

Have a heart of steel and a soul saying "Do it."

It may be that your IDR activities have driven you by their interesting possibilities to the point where you absolutely feel you must design and draft. More often than not, however, composers have to prod themselves a bit in order to move from the IDR phase into drafting and design. It takes courage, for example, to go ahead and begin the composition when you know there are more facts and information that could make it better or even make it acceptable to reviewers. The basic fact about this reason for not doing D and D is that you will never have enough information. Peeking behind the curtain at successful writers will show you that they are never completely satisfied that they have all the information they need. However, prepared writers and composers have done enough IDR to be reasonably sure they are not just giving an opinion about a topic they know nothing or little about. So, they choose to do what they have intended to do all along, organize the mess they made with their IDR by writing/composing.

Designing: Organizing the chaos you made

Design is organizing your composition from the materials you've created during invention, discovery, and research.

A list of possible design and organization elements:

- Maps
- Flow charts
- Titles
- Thesis statements that answer the question "So what?"
- Finding analogies
- Developing a line of reasoning
- Telling the story of your idea
- Finding a centerpiece, visual or otherwise
- Outlines, formal and informal
- Elevator speeches
- Posters and mosaics
- Slide decks

THINKING ALOUD

Out of clutter, find simplicity. From discord, find harmony. In the middle of difficulty lies opportunity.

- Albert Einstein

When you design and draft, be an Einstein.

You will find if you don't know already that setting limits on what you are going to compose and working with those limitations, as well as deciding what is important to write about is a blessing and not a curse. We need limits to be able to predict where we want and need to go, what we want and need to do. In the less academic world of wandering, meditating, and deliberately going on a road trip without a map you can for a time put limits aside if you like. If a class is organized that way, I imagine there will still be deadlines and expectations about sharing your discoveries in some fashion. But academic composing in First-Year Composition, as we pointed out earlier, is building something.

Questions and answers about design

What does a design look like?

Creating an outline is standard for every class, but there are many alternatives and approaches to a design that can work for you personally in the creation of your prototype or draft. Document maps, flow charts, simple topic outlines, sketches with indications of how the sketch organizes your document (Think board games), storyboards, and even digital storytelling or a PowerPoint presentation are all reasonable ways of creating your personal way of revealing what it is you have discovered and how you are going to reveal it.

Is there a place I can start designing?

I imagine you have been designing all along. During the Discovery phase of your project, you began to recognize patterns, associations, and relationships among the clutter and noise of your chaos. You designed already by designing a research agenda, which was a sequence of questions you wanted to answer. In research, one thing found leads you to another. Designing is recognizing a pattern and organizing it in such a way that your audience can follow you through the story of your exploration, the reasoning behind your discovery, or the most or least important of what you found out. If you are testing a hypothesis or doing research with a survey or poll, for example, your design is recommended to you by the protocols for doing the survey or poll. Even though it is recommended and the design is already a part of

THINKING ALOUD

Invention, it must be humbly admitted, does not consist in creating out of void, but out of chaos... the materials must be afforded (on hand)...

- Ann Berthoff

your assignment, it is a good idea to draw up the design or to write down the sequence for yourself.

Conversation Starter

Write a letter to one of the people who you found interesting in your research. In it tell them what you found in their work that was rewarding for you, or interesting, or hard to understand. Use the letter to think about what you want to do in your design. Share this with others and talk about it.

To tell the truth, I tried to find interesting patterns in my discovery phase and wasn't as successful as I think I should have been. What is pattern recognition and how does it work for me in design?

First of all, First-Year Composition classes don't require that you master everything about finding patterns or much of anything else. They do require that you set high standards for yourself and then try to meet them. If you don't meet them, you have not really failed but found out something important. The lower the standard, the less you will find out and the less you learn. Having said that, you are already an expert at pattern recognition by the virtue of being a human being — for example, when you came to class you knew where to go and the sequence of what you had to do to get there. Recognizing a pattern is seeing amid the many elements of information the information that seems to be most related, most associated. It is also understanding how to explain what is reasonable and being able to tell the story of your idea. If you have ever explained anything, given directions, had a discussion or argument that was heated, given an excuse for something to someone you care about, or told a story to anyone, you already are practiced in recognizing and following a pattern to a conclusion.

To paraphrase Kenneth Burke, remember his Parlor analogy in Chapter 1, *form is the arousal and fulfilling of expectations.* Many of the principles for design and organization are based on fulfilling the expectations of the audience.

Editor's Note

Do I get to make up any pattern or design I want?

First, you have to understand what the assignment asks you to do and what the expectations are for your performance. There are academic designs for writing and presentation that are standard formats and that the faculty expect to see. You may be able to mix and match these formats in situations where there is a mixed audience, situations in which interdisciplinary and intercultural work is being done. Still, knowing the basic formats for composition in the various disciplines is an act of joining the club of that discipline and, for a student, an act of self-defense. If you don't know the formats and use them, you are going to fail the class. You can be a rebel, for example, and write a poem instead of a lab report. If the faculty member is willing to tolerate the poem in place of the report, then you are very lucky.

What are the standard formats for academics?

The most common formats are the science report, the humanities report, the argument, the essay, and the format generally accepted for in class written exams and impromptu speeches, the five-paragraph theme. Each one of the formats establishes a way to reasonably explain what you need to explain, make your point, or tell your story in a format acceptable to the academic discipline. The format meets expectations. You can choose to deviate from that format but not without some difficulty and often an explanation. The realities of new technologies and publishing have required everyone to rethink the academic format. Examples of the new formats for communication include blogs, digital storytelling, mosaic designs, and presentation materials suitable for multimedia presentations. Being aware of those formats and the expectations associated with using them must be one of your goals for composition, if only to introduce you to them as ways of alternative communication. Most students have already practiced variations of the new environment and tools for composition as they post on Google+, Facebook, LinkedIn, YouTube, or Twitter.

Conversation Starter

Take a look at the features of Facebook, Google+, or LinkedIn and see if you can design/organize a presentation or paper using the elements you see there. Share with others.

Does my design have to be complicated or pretty?

Good presentations and papers have been designed on a napkin. Also, some really pretty designs have been offered along with some pretty ugly papers. There is a connection between the attention to design and the quality of the performance, but people who are good at writing and composition often have a design already that they use habitually. Many of them, for example, have written enough reports, stories, or essays to have an automatic response ability when they are asked to write something. What often appears as someone who has been given the ability to write by some deity is perhaps more likely someone who has practiced enough to simply shift into gear and get going. It is automatic. Having said that, creating a design that is simple enough to use, clear enough to communicate what you want to do, and reasonably logical will go a long way to improving your chances for an A.

What does reasoning or storytelling have to do with design?

When we say design in D and D, we are referring to the progression of information and ideas through to the conclusion of a composition. It is true that in visual or mixed media presentations you will want to consider visual design as part of what you are doing. But visual design involves the aesthetic appeals in composition and the best means of communicating information. Although there is a connection between the principles of visual design and a design for format and the progression from start to finish, what we mean by design at this point in the process is a focus on a line of reasoning or a plot for the story of your ideas.

THINKING ALOUD

One of the principles of visual design is to work with symmetrical (balanced) designs or asymmetrical (unbalanced) designs in a project such as a poster or ad. What might the idea of working with balanced or unbalanced elements of your paper or presentation mean to you? Is the picture above balanced or asymmetrical?

I noticed that storytelling was in your list of design and organization elements. What does storytelling have to do with academic designs?

If you are arguing, telling a story is an effective way to get your point across (75% more effective than logic according to some). If you are doing a report, using illustrations and giving the story behind your topic ensures you and your audience are literally and figuratively on the same page. So the elements of storytelling are one way to organize your materials and information in a pattern that is useful and recognizable by your audience. Another way to think of it is that topic sentences are like scenes in a play or film. Each scene advances the story, and each paragraph if the paper or presentation is designed well will advance the story of the idea.

Does my design have to be logical?

Probably not, but it must be reasonable unless you are planning to pick a fight. Really, one of the expectations you are expected to fulfill is that not only what you say is reasonable but the way you say it as well. Reasoning in composition is different than logic, although at times you may want to use logical structures such as the syllogism to explain something. A famous example of a syllogism is Socrates is a man. All men are mortal. Therefore, Socrates is mortal. According to Aristotle, this is a demonstration or proof that all men are mortal. (We might ask if women are immortal.) Reasoning, on the other hand, is a way of helping people follow your explanation or argument. *This happens, and then this happens, and then this happens, so I bet this is what will happen next,* would be a template for a line of reasoning. If you don't have a line of reasoning of some form in your presentation you need to explain why you don't want to use one.

Conversation Starter

Try an outline for a line of reasoning with your next design/organization.

I noticed in your list you included an elevator speech and a question — "So what?" What's an elevator speech and why ask "So What?" It seems cynical to me.

Unless the context is clear, the "so what" question is cynical and might be taken as insulting. What we want to think about when we are working with our composition is perhaps a more useful question that addresses the same thing: *If I believe what I have discovered, what difference does it make to what I think or what I do and what difference should it make to an audience?* This is one way to figure out not only why you want to tell people about your discovery but helps you understand what you want your audience to do. It also helps you identify why the audience might be interested in what you have to say, which helps you sharpen your focus in design. A rule of thumb: Keep the audience in mind.

If you write out your own answer to that question you will have a thesis statement started and, perhaps, an elevator speech, which is what you would tell people your project is about if you were riding in an elevator with them. (I usually say five floors on an elevator that moves steadily but not too quickly.)

Assignment for Designing and Organizing

Create a presentation to a group or the class in which you present a design for your project that explains your points of interest or your line of reasoning, or presents the story of your idea. Share it and use responses to sharpen your presentation/document.

Drafting: Putting it together in one place

How should I start drafting?

Until you are practiced, writing a draft is often like starting a cold car during an early Minnesota winter morning. It takes some juice. Your design may have given you a jumpstart. Many times we can finish a design and find we are already writing or that we start writing halfway through the design and organization process. If you have been keeping a journal about your research or writing in a sketchbook or notebook, you have already been drafting. The IDR process provides you with materials and starts and stops at paragraphs and sentences, which helps you identify possible thesis statements and topics for paragraphs. If you are stuck in any way starting a draft go to your notes and research information. Start with something, anything, if you have to. The point is that you need to write enough to get that car started. Another way to get started is to begin with a quote and start explaining what the quote means to you.

> Drafting is using language to invent and discover. Using words and naming things makes us participants in the world.
>
> **Editor's Note**

Conversation Starter

Answer the following: Is drafting more like sailing, fishing, climbing, or riding a trail bike for you? Explain why.

THINKING ALOUD

Your task is not to reveal the Truth, which would suggest you have direct connections to a deity. Your task is to maintain truthfulness, meaning that what you offer your audience is as truthful an interpretation of your discovery as possible. To be truthful a composition needs to make sense, have a line of reasoning, give illustrations, tell a story we can follow, fulfill our expectations, and not bore us. If a draft suggests a composer is attempting at least some of these things, we will probably accept it as truthful.

> The trick with working with an outline is not to insist on following it exactly. As you draft, you will want to monitor and adjust the outline when you have the draft done, since the writing itself will suggest other patterns and other materials you haven't thought were important to you but are.
>
> **Editor's Note**

Use a prompt to get started — a prompt is an assignment either someone else gives you or that you give yourself. Do a 20-minute timed writing — the only rule is that you must keep writing for 20 minutes without stopping. Other ways to get started are:

- Begin in the middle.
- Interview yourself about the topic.
- Begin with why the is important to you.
- Begin with why it is important to the audience/reader.
- Begin with writing the opposite of what you believe or feel about the topic and then write a response to what you wrote.
- Put a working title on a blank piece of paper and just respond to what it makes you think of and feel.
- Write an elevator speech.

I'm afraid I will get stuck. What do I do?

All the draft starters above are also good for getting unstuck. The term "writer's block" is like a ghost in the attic for most writers and composers. Sometimes you need to just relax and walk around a bit if you get stuck. Sometimes you have to work through the problem that is keeping you from going on. The key is to relax into the draft enough that being stuck is not going to create so much stress you can't continue. If so, you will need to get away from the process. Don't take anything too seriously during a draft. You get to say dumb things and take them back without people knowing if you want. Throw a picture into the draft if you need to write about something other than what you have written about. Your multimodal approach for

THINKING ALOUD

Use the rhetorical appeals as a rubric to start your drafting: your background and relation to the topic (ethos), what you think is a line of reasoning for the topic (logos), how you feel about the topic (pathos). There is a fourth appeal that Aristotle leaves out of the rhetoric but takes up in a separate work — story (mythos). I like to think of mythos as the long lost brother or sister of the other three. What is the story you want to tell?

THINKING ALOUD

Writing is itself invention, invention with words. No matter how organized we think we are, unless we are into working with words and love them in some way, we will get stuck and find moving difficult. If you want to keep drafting, define something or choose a word from a thesaurus that you like for any reason. Let your language lead you on as much as the design.

your research and discovery will have provided you with pictures, quotes, songs, and any of these things can and will come to your aid if you need them. Mostly, remember that you are the director, el jefe, the one in charge. How can your draft be wrong when you are the boss of it?

What if I know I am being stupid or not writing what I want to?

Attitude check: don't write something you don't want to unless someone is paying you to do it. Also, remember your passion and that we are all beginners at something. Even if you couldn't write at all, it wouldn't necessarily mean you are stupid. Also, failure with a draft is an option. In *Exploiting Chaos: 150 Ways to Spark Innovation during Times of Change*, Jeremy Gutsche says that bosses should fire people who don't make mistakes.

A draft is a reasonable attempt to organize and tell the story of your discovery. If you come back to it after a failed attempt and try again, it is usually clearer because you know what you don't want to do. If you're perfect every time you start a draft, you aren't really composing — you must be copying something. Half of success with communicating in general and with composing in particular is the willingness to look silly or stupid. Most of the time we are in good company when we do.

Finally, remember why you are writing something. You are adding to knowledge and advocating for something that is important to you. It usually has something to do with your culture and the people you believe to be "your people." To have a chance to say something for those we love and respect is something exciting enough to keep us drafting and following through to the end.

Assignment for Drafting

Write a draft of a paper/presentation for any one of your assignments. You will be doing this a lot in First-Year Composition.

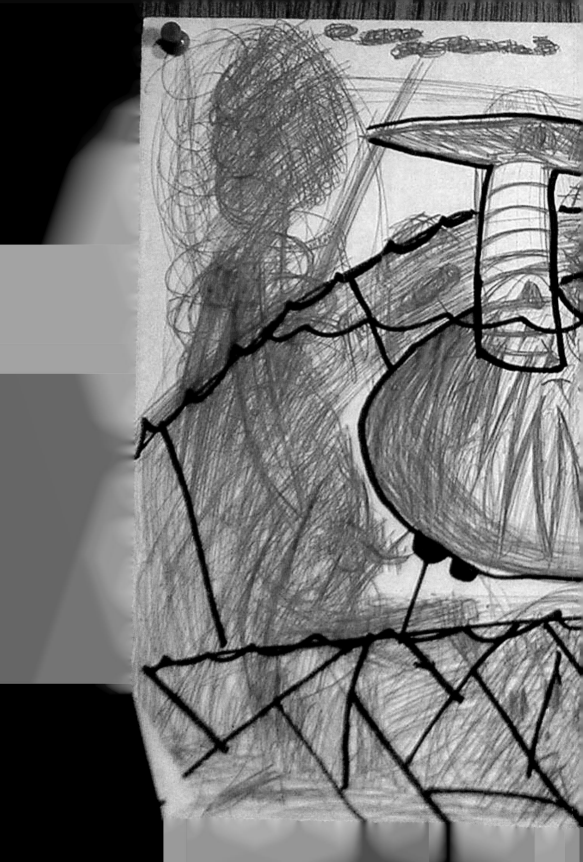

REVISION, REWRITING, AND EDITING

The human mind may not be much suited to logic at all . . . but is well suited to judging the fairness of social bargins and the sincerity of social offers.

- Matt Ridley

Like all composition, the experience of revising, rewriting, and editing are social experiences, and participating in class reviews and workshops, and responding to faculty feedback are the most important skills to learn. When you revise, rewrite, and edit, you are creating something you can be proud of.

Get the most out of your draft (prototype).

USE this chapter. It is the most obvious of tool kits and instruments to remake your draft (prototype). Prototypes and Betas are made to be tested and improved. It's no different with a draft. Once you open the chapter, tools will be arranged for your use in specific tasks. Because the tools and instruments are tested for you, they are ready to use. In this part of your journey from invention to submission, you get to focus on elements of composition such as style, emphasis in text and design, and readability. This is the time to ask yourself questions and find answers about what your audience reads and sees in your document.

> We can remake the world daily.
>
> - Paul Wellstone

One of the surprises for First-Year Composition students is how much time is invested in working with a draft — revision, rewriting, and editing. You know you are missing the spirit of FYC if you find yourself wanting to write something once and be done with it. To get the spirit, the one that says "Do it," we recommend an attitude check. The idea that a paper is finished when a composer has drafted it and run it through a spell check is an idea spawned in hurry-up academic settings in English classes and in other classes where writing is necessary. For example, how many times did you write something once and hand it in? The habit isn't any better in the sciences than in the humanities. Lab reports seldom get a composer's treatment.

Why revise and rewrite?

Working with a draft will improve your grade, sometimes dramatically. More can be learned about composition during the revision, rewriting, and editing phases about writing and composing than at any other phase.

Although the writing process is recursive and you have been revising, rewriting, and editing all along, working with a draft allows you dedicated time for improving your performance and product.

Belonging in your community is important to you. Working with a draft engages you in shop talk, the indication that you are indeed part of the scholarly community and a composer/writer — the more you do it, the more you sense you belong in the community of scholars.

Fundamental questions are: "Am I being truthful, and have I interested the reader?" Often, understanding your pattern or progress in your draft is to think of it as storytelling with the story of an idea as its core. What is the story you are telling? How does your story relate to stories your audience like to hear?

THINKING ALOUD

Despite... differences in a story's style or convention or form, storytelling per se is a fundamental human enterprise because storytelling sustains all of our relationships, both individually and communally. In keeping up with our friends, we are keeping up with their stories and telling our own; the value of a old friend is inseparable from the common fund of stories so incessantly mined in making sense of the moment. To get to know someone new is above all to engage in that tentative or excited exchange of stories.

- Catherine Wallace

Revision

Go analog at some point in the revision process. It is best in revision to start there so you can see the whole composition.

The purpose of revision is to consider the progression of ideas, your story line, or your pattern in regard to readability and coherence.

Revision suggests working with the larger features of your design. If you imagine your paper or presentation as a dark yard, your job is to string small lights across the yard in such a way that a guest could find where you want them to go. In revision, you make sure your lights are placed in the right way and that they are all lit.

In order to do this, you will want to read and have others read what you have in order to see better how you can help the audience follow your line of reasoning, your story plot, or your pattern of explanation. Revision often requires working with segments of your project, written or visual, adding some and taking others out. It also asks you to provide the transitions between segments of your composition so that readers can more easily recognize when you are going someplace different and the relationship of that new place to where they are at the moment in their reading or viewing.

Tasks for revision:

- Check to see if the composition meets the requirements of the assignment and change the composition to relate it directly to the assignment.

- Create a possible clearer design.
- Add transition sentences or other directions.
- Find some way of checking to see if your directions intended to help the audience follow you are clear. You need an audience at this point to tell you, and it helps to get both peer and faculty feedback.
- Move segments and paragraphs to work better with your reasoning for your design. Sometimes your final paragraph will work better as your first.
- Write an elevator speech for a summary of what you are trying to do.
- Check to see if your peers and faculty understand what it is you want to say and for them to do and making necessary additions.
- Take out larger sections of the composition, paragraphs, segments, or even pages that seem to lead people away from what you are doing.
- Add any data, resources, visuals, or information that help illustrate your point of view or highlight something you believe should be emphasized.

Conversation Starter

You will not get to use all the revision tools and instruments in the list, and the list is by no means everything you could do to revise. It's important to read your draft and have others read it while considering the list in order to choose something that will improve your composition. This is often done is a workshop in class, usually called a peer review.

Peer responses at this point in the process are usually directed to wanting to know why you said something or how one thing relates to another — for example: How come? How do you know that? I don't get it? I would like to know more about this? Whoa, back up. I don't understand? What do you mean by that? Why did they do that? So, one way to revise is to make a list of reader questions, either questions you anticipate or questions that are asked by peer reviewers or the faculty.

THINKING ALOUD

One of the more popular assignments in FYC is the rhetorical analysis assignment in which writers analyze a document, an ad, a picture, or a film and write about it. One assignment that would be useful in regard to revision would be to exchange papers with each other and spend at least an hour doing the same kind of rhetorical analysis for your classmates as you did or will do in a rhetorical analysis paper. Sharing the analysis is of course useful in revision and rewriting, but doing the analysis will help you understand what the composer is trying to do better as well as what you might do better after your analysis of his or her composition.

Conversation Starter

It's clear that since the revolution of the new technologies for composition and communication, the world of the classroom for composition has changed. One big change is obvious even in this book. The text in this box, for example, could be naked text. You might read it because you are involved in the process of revision, but we know that often only the most dedicated will read most of the text we write, and we know that visuals and presentation design increases the number of readers who will stay with the text and, therefore, get more out of it.

Naked text

Presentation is therefore an important consideration for revision. Consider the visual elements for a revision of your draft.

Revised as a tweet

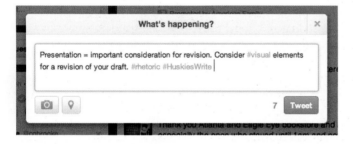

Revised as a flyer

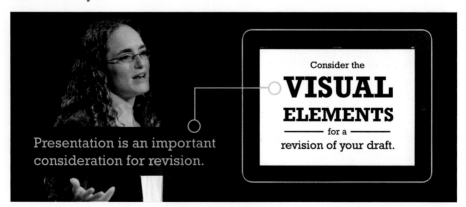

Rewriting

Revision is usually considered an "overhaul" of the paper where the writer moves blocks of material around and either adds or cuts material. Rewriting often refers to working on paragraphs. A playwright will often make a journal by printing pages and pasting them onto a sketchbook or notebook in order to write, edit, and revise during rehearsals. Using a tool like this is useful for writers and composers as well.

There are some aspects about the physical requirements for rewriting that require your attention. Work old school during a rewrite. Research shows that unless your work with a hard copy of your work you will miss about 20% of what you need to find out. In other words, rewriting, including editing, requires you to at some point print a copy and look at it in analog form as well as digital. Resistance is futile. Print your draft.

One thing to remember about rewriting, especially in rewriting paragraphs, is to make a gloss at the side of any paragraph about what you wanted to get across in the paragraph. Doing this will lead you to ask the question: "What might happen if I put it this way, or added this thought, or summarized this sentence?" Those questions asked and answered by you will go a long way to improve clarity in your composition.

THINKING ALOUD

One way to check your draft to see if it is revealing the pattern you want and reasonable is to ask yourself and then answer for yourself with the help of others: What does this paragraph do at this point in the composition, or what does this visual do? Why am I placing the paragraph or visual at this particular place in my composition? Is there a better place?

Rewriting tools and instruments

Rewrite to focus

Every piece of writing should have a dominant meaning, and although good writing has depth and texture, something should predominate.

- Rewrite to define and name concepts that seem too abstract. Definition is one of the best ways to work with terms or ideas that seem out of reach for the audience. Most definitions are in need of an illustration or an example so that the audience knows how you are using the term or concept.
- Provide the information or piece of the story that is missing that is leading to misunderstanding. *Ethymeme* is the rhetorical version of logic's syllogism. A syllogism describes a logical progression from one idea to the next. Remember the syllogism: Socrates is a man. All men are mortal. Socrates is mortal. The enthymeme would be Socrates is a man. All men are mortal. The second part of the syllogism is left out. This is the natural way for people to talk and write. What this requires is that people need to "fill in the blank" with cultural knowledge. A good example of how this works is the statement that "I know Mary was at the movie last night because her lamb was there." If someone has not read "Mary Had a Little Lamb" or had it said to them by a family member when they were young, or heard the song by Stevie Ray Vaughn, the idea that the lamb was at the movies and it proved Mary was there is impossible to understand. (If you saw *Dusk Til Dawn* you also heard Los Lobos do this song.) Thus, one way to rewrite something in regard to understanding is to find the cultural knowledge that is necessary for an audience to understand what you are getting at.
- Re-read your draft and your elevator speech. See if they match up. In a science report, the elevator speech may be your abstract.
- The focus starts with the title, look at your working title to see if it indeed directs the reader as you intend.
- State the dominant meaning in a sentence or two. If you can't, there is no focus.
- In order to find the focus you want, answer the following questions:
  - What do you want the reader to remember?
  - What is one thing the reader needs to know?

- What idea would you like to explore during revision?
- What single message would you like the final draft to deliver?

Once you find your focus and can write it down in a sentence or two, you then rewrite to keep that focus in mind. In short, if someone asks you what something is doing in the composition, you should be able to explain it in terms of your focus.

Rewrite to collect

Rewriting to collect is finding information that needs to be in the essay.

- To see if you need more information, go through your essay and put a check in the margin whenever you find specific information.
- Kinds of specific information are quotes, revealing detail, facts, statistics, anecdotes, first hand observations, precise definitions, authoritative citations, or references.

185

- There is no quota of information necessary, but if you have pages of writing without specific information, you will need to collect (research) and add some.
- In fact, one reason to do research after IDR is to add specific information to your writing.

If you are stuck at any point during the writing process, research gives you ideas for writing in the first place.

Rewrite with appeals in mind:

Aristotle's classic appeals are the character of the writer in the composition, the logic used to explain and argue, and the emotional appeals in use of language (we must add visuals). To this we add the story told in the composition. What story are you telling? Add to this the following:

Advertising's 15 Basic Appeals
(From "Mass Advertising as Social Forecast")

Jib Fowles

1. *Need for sex* - Surprisingly, Fowles found that only 2 percent of the television ads, he surveyed used this appeal. It may be too blatant, he concluded, and often detracts from the product.
2. *Need for affiliation* - The largest number of ads use this approach: "Are you looking for friendship?" Advertisers can also use this negatively, to make you worry that you'll lose friends if you don't use a certain product.
3. *Need to nurture* - Every time you see a puppy, a kitten or a child, the appeal is to your paternal or maternal instincts.
4. *Need for guidance* - A father or mother figure can appeal to your desire for someone to care for you, so you won't have to worry. Betty Crocker is a good example.

---

5. ***Need to aggress*** - We all have had a desire to get even, and some ads give you this satisfaction.
6. ***Need to achieve*** - The ability to accomplish something difficult and succeed identifies the product with winning. Sports figures as spokespersons project this image.
7. ***Need to dominate*** - The power we lack is what we can look for in a commercial to "master the possibilities."
8. ***Need for prominence*** - We want to be admired and respected; to have high social status. Tasteful china and classic diamonds offer this potential.
9. ***Need for attention*** - We want people to notice us; we want to be looked at. Cosmetics are a natural for this approach.
10. ***Need for autonomy*** - Within a crowded environment, we want to be singled out, to be a "breed apart." This can also be used negatively: you may be left out if you don't use a particular product.
11. ***Need to escape*** - Flight is very appealing; you can imagine adventures you cannot have; the idea of escape is pleasurable.
12. ***Need to feel safe*** - To be free from threats, to be secure is the appeal of many insurance and bank ads.
13. ***Need for aesthetic sensations*** - Beauty attracts us, and classic art or dance makes us feel creative, enhanced.
14. ***Need to satisfy curiosity*** - Facts support our belief that information is quantifiable and numbers and diagrams make our choices seem scientific.
15. ***Psychological needs*** - Fowles defines sex (item no.1) as a biological need, and so he classifies our need to sleep, eat, and drink in this category. Advertisers for juicy pizza are especially appealing late at night.

Consider whether you are using an appeal that is obvious and directive — a *hot* appeal — or a *cool* appeal that is subtle and inviting. Add one hot or one cool appeal through language or visuals.

Rewriting for voice and work with style

Rewriting for voice has to do with working with style. As Douglas LeBlanc puts it: "Style is a way of writing. It results in a particular feel to a sentence, a paragraph, a composition. Dull, punchy, artificial, melodramatic, sharp, crisp, clear, convoluted, and a whole host of other adjectives can be called upon to describe a particular piece of writing."

The way to make your style more appealing or the ethos in your composition more attractive is to work on your style. Working on style doesn't have to be painful but often is for FYC students because it requires a lot of rewriting. If you want to know more about style, most handbooks and sites such as our LEO (Literacy Education Online) from the Write Place, offer help with wordiness, bothersome vocabulary, and how punctuation or the use of pronouns affects your style.

Rewriting for style often takes a self-imposed assignment or one from your faculty. Here's an example:

1. Choose a paragraph. It should be at least five sentences long. You may work on the rewrite with a partner. However, everyone should hand in a paragraph of their own. (Hand in both the original and the rewrite.)
2. Cut six words. (You're looking for deadwood and repetition.)
3. Cut all but two modifiers. (Adjectives and adverbs)
4. Add two action verbs. (For examples of action verbs for ideas, see the verb list.)
5. Write a transition sentence at the end of the paragraph that will lead the reader into the next paragraph.
6. For fun, add one word other than English. (You decide if you should translate its meaning.)
7. Add a logical marker such as "therefore," "consequently," or "thus."
8. Rewrite the beginnings of one or two sentences. Start with a noun or pronoun.
9. Add an analogy or a metaphor.
10. Write a short reflection or evaluation of your experience. What do you think of the new paragraph? What was the hardest thing to do? Explain why you chose to change something in the paragraph? (Write this following the rewrite of the paragraph.)

Editing as rewriting

Editing is a form of rewriting and it has a place in the processes of composing, especially when a composer is getting ready to submit a final paper or presentation. There are editors and composers who specialize in usage and grammar. Often the image of an English major is that of an editor on an error hunt. In reality, the rubric for assessing your work in the English Department includes usage and grammar, but only for 10%. Composers who are successful, however, recognize that editing their work is essential, since there are times when errors interfere with a reader or audience's ability to appreciate and understand the composition. This is the most important reason for rewriting as an editor in regard to surface errors and standards of usage.

The most common errors in usage:

- Missing comma after an introductory element
- Vague pronoun reference
- Missing comma in a compound sentence
- Wrong word
- Missing comma(s) with a nonrestrictive element
- Wrong or missing verb ending
- Wrong or missing preposition
- Comma splice
- Missing or misplaced possessive apostrophe
- Unnecessary shift in tense
- Unnecessary shift in pronoun
- Sentence fragment
- Wrong tense or verb form
- Lack of subject-verb agreement
- Missing comma in a series
- Lack of agreement between pronoun and antecedent
- Unnecessary comma(s) with a restrictive element
- Fused sentence
- Misplaced or dangling modifier

(By Lunsford and Conners)

Conversation Starter

There are some errors that will creep into your writing no matter what, and finding ways to review for them and edit is the way to be a good composer. What you can do with Lunsford and Conners's list is to review the editorial comments during peer reviews and during faculty feedback and pick the top five surface errors you repeatedly make. Study in a handbook or a handout from the Write Place what those errors mean and how to fix them. Use the list as a way of editing your own work and give it to your peers during review to look specifically for those errors. This is the kind of "error hunt" that can pay off in regard to actually reducing the number of errors in your final papers and presentations.

Review to check for citation format and work cited format. Whether it is MLA, APA, or another style sheet commonly used in your area of study, almost all academic papers require citations and either a bibliography or works cited page. Practicing citation during your entire FYC class is one way to get into the habit of giving credit. Handbooks, LEO, and OWL are useful, plus you can go right to the original source and go to the MLA website or the APA website.

Peer groups

One of the most common aspects of education in the US is the idea of working in groups. It's surprising therefore that we don't spend much time thinking about what happens in those groups and how we can make them more useful. Mainly, we get so used to working in small groups that we take the process for granted. The best kinds of editing work can be done within small groups of peers who understand each other's problems. The key with peer groups is to focus on the task at hand as often as possible.

Are there basic rules of conduct for peer groups? Yes, and no. Peers often find informal ways of accomplishing formal tasks. Still, there are some basic guidelines.

The point of the group is to help the writer understand the paper better and to improve. People have to be willing to take risks and to say what they believe. They also have to be willing to listen carefully and to be open minded. The members have to stay on task for a reasonable amount of time. Considering the following a rules of thumb or guidelines for review peer groups:

- Be willing to listen and listen carefully both as the composer and as a group member.
- Offer the group something to look for in your paper.
- Discuss the issues and problems of fixing the paper. As a group member you will not only want to point out places you believe should be fixed, but you will want to explain why you feel there is a problem. Offer specific suggestions whenever possible.
- Vary the process:
  - Pass papers around.
  - Read papers out loud.
  - Break up into groups of three and read individual paragraphs.
  - Decide in advance to look for some aspect of writing that is interesting and that might lead to surface problems. For example, looking at the verbs in a paper often leads to other discoveries about style and sentence structure.
  - Have peers take turns asking the writer *specific* questions about why he or she did something.

Assignment for Designing and Organizing

In reviewing your draft for any project, select from the tools in the chapter and create a list of revision, rewriting, and editing tools you find particularly useful. Put that list with every draft you write and use it to work with peers and faculty.

ASSESSMENT, EVALUATION, AND GRADING

These people who can see right through you never quite do you justice, because they never give you credit for the effort you're making to be better than you actually are, which is difficult and well meant and deserving of some little notice.

- Marilynne Robinson

Composers as well as athletes know coaches must offer criticism and advice, as well as demonstrations of exercises and game strategy. For a composer as well as an athlete, setting a personal record is the goal each time out. Assessment, evaluation, and grading measure your shot at a personal best and allow a discussion that follows your performance.

You don't always get what you want, so try hard to get what you need.

The paraphrase of the Rolling Stones song lyrics hits the right nerve in working with assessment and evaluation — judgment. The word *judgment* is unnerving because it calls up images and feelings of being judged, often in situations where we feel we have been misunderstood. Our experiences with judgment often do not match up with the expectation of those kinder sounding words, assessment, and evaluation. The key to getting prepared for judgment and the grade that comes with it is to have done what the process helps us do: Work together to create the best possible document or documents so that misunderstandings about what you are doing and why are rare and not the norm. All along you have responded to evaluations and assessments in reviews and comments from your faculty. If you have, what comes in grades will not be a surprise or that frightening. What you need, now, is the confirmation of what you expect from your efforts, based on what you have found out already.

> The relationship between effort and the assessment of results is not only hard to define but not fair to everyone in the class. Your assessment will most likely be made on the assumption that everyone is working hard in the class.

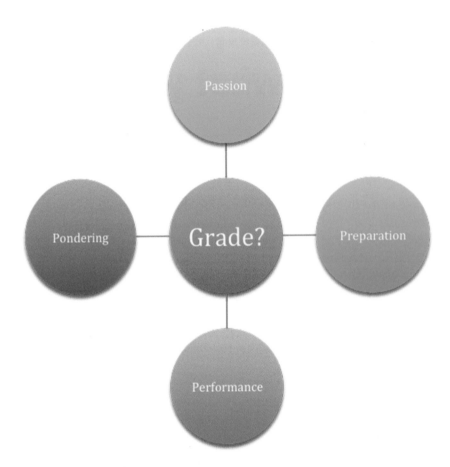

Getting ready for assessment, evaluation, and grading

All of **Huskies Write** is dedicated to your success, and part of that success is getting the best possible grade in your FYC class. The grade is only part of the success, but generally the grade stands for faculty's assessment of your passion, preparation, performance, and pondering. Your submitted papers and presentations stand as a demonstration of those four essential elements of success.

If you ask students why they are taking a class, they will often answer, first, to get a grade. Although this is the most obvious answer for some, getting a grade in a composition class is only one way to assess your progress or lack of it. Writing involves the social interaction in the review, discussion, and evaluation of research, drafts, revisions, and final versions of papers. Learning to work with both faculty and peer feedback is a major part of your experience in beginning composition. Peer editing workshops, conferences with faculty, and the more formal reviews when students receive a grade are all part of the learning experience.

But if you are not prepared for the assessment phase of the writing process, you can get sidetracked and forget why you are doing what you are doing, which is practicing the arts and sciences of becoming a scholar in order to join the scholarly community. Along the way, you will gain skills in composing that make you a better thinker, communicator, and student. The most obvious sidetrack to pull out on for a composer/scholar is getting a grade he or she finds less than satisfactory. Rather than focusing on the benefits of assessment and improving, students can get caught in a loop where they see grade failure as the defining experience rather than learning or getting better. Of course the irony is that to get a better grade students have to fail sometimes in order to learn. In fact, we often learn as much if not more from our failures than successes. In addition, research on learning suggests that unless we fail we do not learn.

Conversation Starter

Make a list of failures in writing and composition on the right side of a piece of paper. Draw a line down the middle. On the other side of the line make a list of things you learned from it or things you might have learned if you had thought about it. Talk this over with your classmates.

The most common question asked regarding assessment and grading:

The question asked most often in class when students are concerned about how they are going to be graded is: "How many pages do you want?" The question seems troublesome to faculty because it is the one question they have all heard again and again. Faculty often think that the student is either attempting to do the minimum of work for an assignment they know is important or that the student hasn't read the syllabus, which often has page length as one of the criteria.

Always submit your document or presentation to meet the deadline set by the assignment. If you feel you are not ready to submit, remember that no composition is finished, it is only abandoned.

Editor's Note

If we do an analysis of why papers or documents are expected to be a certain length, we come up with the following context and possible answer:

1. The English Department has a requirement of 20 pages of polished work for each student during the semester.
2. We all know that writers and composers will write a lot more than 20 pages.
3. The fact of university writing is that the faculty will not and should not read everything you write. In fact, if someone is reading everything

THINKING ALOUD

Make failure something you do every day. Make reflecting on your failure a habit every day. Be successful every day. Make reflecting on your successes a habit.

you write, you are not writing enough. You might, considering journal writing and drafting, write 20 or more pages to get 5 for your final submission for a grade.

4. Most First-Year Composition classes have paper page requirements of 3 to 5, 5 to 7, or 7 to 12 pages in length, and although the faculty will be aware that the total number of pages should add up to 20, there may actually be many more because 20 pages is intended to be a minimum standard for polished text in a class.

5. Most FYC classes require shorter papers because faculty want you to practice various formats, and a semester is actually short. The practice, for example, in many high school classes is to spend the semester writing a long research paper and practicing all the note taking, research, and drafting skills by focusing on one format. Students sometimes blow off shorter papers at the start of a composition class because they believe "the important stuff" is coming later.

6. Because some formats naturally require more pages, such as a science report format, the length of a paper will depend on how you follow the format and how you manage to make it precise enough to fit into the requirements of the course.

7. If you are asked to work with multimodal approaches and presentations rather than the standard "naked text," the page number question becomes harder to answer since, according to Jason Tham, a composer should estimate two pages of composition for every page of naked text.

"How long should it be?" As you can see it does depend on the context of the assignment, your format and design, and your inclusion of visuals. Also, the analysis suggests to you that page length does have something to do with your grade. If you haven't thought through the elements of the page length question, it is very possible you could be surprised by a grade.

Conversation Starter

Use the tear-out rubric sheet to talk about grades and assessment for papers in your class. Trade papers with someone and following the criteria give them a grade. Discuss your assessment in groups and with your faculty member.

Assessment, Evaluation, Grading

Assignment criteria and grading criteria

There is a tear-out sheet for the assessment criteria for the English Department that explains what a student should be able to do when they are finished taking our classes. The criteria is an essential criteria for FYC, but assessment and grading are done with the understanding that some of you are beginning more than others. In short, the faculty will cut you some slack but are serious about the standards set by the criteria. The best piece of advice for doing well and being prepared for the assessment is to know the assignment inside and out.

If you want to know how you will be graded (assessed), study and ask enough questions about the assignment to be ready for the grade and comments. Simply, a composition that does not fall within the boundaries of the assignment will not do well at all. Examples of misunderstandings and attempts to write outside of assignment boundaries are many and painful. One example is a student who wrote a good review of a Johnny Cash record and submitted it as a biography. The student spent weeks arguing that the review could indeed be interpreted as a biography and eventually passed but with a much lower grade than he could have had because of all the time he wasted arguing a point that he was stuck on while the rest of the class moved on. The lesson to be learned here is get permission at the beginning for any modifications of the criteria for the assignment. If you can't make your case for composing "outside" the box before you get too far into the process, the chances of making your case later are nearly zero.

Meeting deadlines is essential to your success. In order to stay up with deadlines and faculty expectations remember that the faculty member has the option to monitor and adjust to the needs of the class as a whole and change anything in the syllabus in regard to material and deadlines. Those changes will be communicated, usually on D2L or by e-mail as well as an announcement in class. If you don't look for them or have missed a class and don't pay attention to any changes, chances are you will suffer a disappointment.

Editor's Note

Four common assignments

What you expect to write and some calibration regarding what is commonly submitted for an FYC class is an important way of getting the most out of assessment. The following are the four most common assignments.

> **Conversation Starter**
>
> The four assignments reveal the pattern for the assignments you will be given: A context for the assignment, directions for completing the assignment, and grading criteria. Identify the elements of the pattern for each of the following assignments. In addition, write up questions about the assignment that you might like to ask the faculty member or members that created it. However, some faculty may be using other genre and will provide class-specific assignments. Reading student models is also helpful. If you need them, most faculty members have saved examples of good student writing.

Essay

The historical meaning of an essay is "an attempt," suggesting it is a speculative kind of writing. It is also the genre of writing most associated with the idea of you giving your opinion about something, usually following a relaxed line of reasoning or telling a story to illustrate some point that you are passionate about. An essay is often thought of as an editorial, and indeed an editorial can be an essay. The most common essay types are editorials (opinion pieces), narratives, descriptions, extended definitions, autobiographies, and biographies. In each case, the line drawn between the essay, an argument, or an exposition is a very narrow line. Your instructor may ask you to do research for an essay.

One of the bits of advice about essays is "Show; don't tell." One of the problems with storytelling and narrative in FYC is the tyranny of chronological time. Often a writer will begin a story and find that every minute in a week intrudes into the paper, and there is no end to the details or way of selecting details. In short, an essay is not usually simply a matter of recording something that happened as you might want to in a news article, but rather it is driven in some way by an idea and a central incident that means something to you.

Assignment 1:
Letter to the Editor

Tone: Personal/Professional; first- or third-person point of view (POV)

Audience: The editor-in-chief of *University Chronicle* and general readers

Length: 750-1,200 words

Purpose: To offer your professional opinion on a recent issue or ongoing event. Bring the editor's attention to matters that deserve immediate attention.

Assignment: Newspaper columns and editorial pages are particularly good places for your opinion to be heard. They are immediate, timely, and adaptable. For this assignment, you will write to the chief editor of our school's publication, the *University Chronicle*, addressing an issue or event that is deserving of the local public's attention (such as the safety issues, allocation of student activity fees, student welfare, academic support, employee benefits, campus activities, campus services, policies, etc.). The topic you pick should be debatable and interesting for the SCSU community (students, faculty, and staff). You should also choose a topic that is not constantly rehashed in the media: you may not do this assignment on abortion, gun control, or the smoking ban. Support your stance with facts and evidence. Don't be vague in any of your claims. Before your start writing, do some research to get background information about the your topic. Be clear in your language.

You may use first-person POV, but remember, the opinion isn't just about you; the topic is the hero. In your rhetorical analysis, you analyzed how public speakers and advertisers used rhetorical appeals (ethos, pathos, logos, and mythos) and alternative rhetorical device (metaphor, irony, enthymeme) to persuade. Now the tables have turned and you are the one making an argument. Make thoughtful choices in choosing rhetorical appeals and devices to make a strong argument. End with a strong call to action.

Format: Refer to the features of a commentary in *Writing Today*. To supplement, you should also look at existing letters to the editor on the *University Chronicle* website. Visit www.universitychronicle.net. Then, hover over the "Opinions" tab and click on "Letters to the Editor," as shown in the screenshot below:

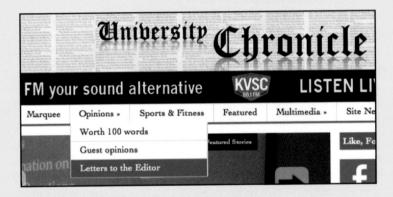

Opportunity for publication: Upon submission of your final draft, the instructor will provide feedback to your essay and recommend that you submit your work for possible publication in the *Chronicle* if it is well written. You have an opportunity to complete your homework and be published (which looks great on your résumé), so put your full effort into this assignment.

Reports

Reporting information and explaining it is not simply gathering a batch of material and placing it on paper. It is an attempt to understand something and requires interpreting information in light of a point of view. There are many formats for reports, but one of the most common is a scientific report that follows a specific pattern with an abstract, introduction, review of literature, a description of the method of research, findings of the research, and a conclusion. The English Department's focal point for reports is articulating and developing critical and analytical perspectives in writing using researched evidence.

Assignment 2:
Report

Write a report about what you find out regarding campus involvement at SCSU. The purpose of the report is to help your follow classmates and other new students to find what is interesting and what might involve them in campus life. Keep in mind our discussions about this topic, especially the idea that campus involvement often translates into academic success. In your report follow what is known as a format for most science reports, although this report does not focus on an experiment but mostly secondary materials from your book of readings and campus websites.

Title Page: The essential information here is your name, the title of the project, and the date. Be aware of any other information your instructor requires. The title of a report can be a statement of the subject. An effective title is informative but reasonably short. Ornamental or misleading titles may annoy readers.

Abstract or Summary: This section states the report in miniature. It summarizes the whole report in one concise paragraph of about 100-200 words. It might be useful to think in terms of writing one sentence to summarize each of the traditional report divisions: objective, method, discussion, and conclusions. Emphasize the objective (which states the problem) and the analysis of the results (including recommendations). Avoid the temptation to copy a whole paragraph from elsewhere in your report and make it do double duty. Since the abstract condenses and emphasizes the most important elements of the whole report, you cannot write it until after you have completed the report. Remember, the abstract should be a precise and specific summary — give details. A technical document is not a mystery novel — give your conclusion right away. Support it later.

Introduction: Whereas the abstract summarizes the whole report, the introduction of a technical report identifies the subject, the purpose (or objective), and the plan of development of the report. The subject is the "what," the purpose is the "why," and the plan is the "how." Together these acquaint the reader with the problem you are setting out to solve. State the subject and purpose as clearly and concisely as possible, usually in one sentence called the thesis or purpose statement. Use the introduction to provide the reader with any background information the reader will need before you can launch into the body of your paper. You may have to define the terms used in stating the subject and provide background such as theory or history of the subject. For example, the purpose statement quoted above might warrant some explanation of daylight trawling or even of the commercial shrimp industry. Avoid the tendency to use the introduction merely to fill space with sweeping statements that are unrelated to the specific purpose of your report ("Throughout the ages, human beings have looked up at the stars and wondered about [your topic here].").

Background or Review of Literature: If the introduction requires a large amount of supporting information, such as a review of literature or a description of a process, then the background material should form its own section. This section may include a review of previous research, or formulas the reader needs to understand the problem. In an academic report, it is also the point where you can show your comprehension of the problem.

Discussion: This section is the most important part of your report. It takes many forms and may have subheadings of its own. Its basic components are methods, findings (or results), and evaluation (or analysis). In a progress report, the methods and findings may dominate; a final report should emphasize evaluation. Most academic assignments should also focus on your evaluation of the subject. Before you begin writing, ask the journalist's questions: Who? When? Where? What? Why? How? The last three in particular will help you focus analysis. Beyond asking these simple questions, you also need to make decisions such as: How do you interpret the data? What is the significance of your findings?

Conclusion: What knowledge comes out of the report? As you draw a conclusion, you need to explain it in terms of the preceding discussion. Some repetition of the most important ideas you presented there is expected, but you should avoid copying.

Recommendations: What actions does the report call for? The recommendations should be clearly connected to the results of the rest of the report. You may need to make those connections explicit at this point — your reader should not have to guess at what you mean. This section may also include plans for how further research should proceed. In professional writing, this section often comes immediately after the introduction.

References: Use either MLA or APA citation and reference format (Works Cited or Reference page). Refer to the citation format materials in your LEO handouts and refer as well to MLA or APA websites for more detailed information on how to cite.

Rhetorical analysis

A rhetorical analysis is one of the most assigned papers because its purpose is to think critically and thoughtfully about the persuasive elements of a document, film, picture, movie, or just about anything that we can examine rhetorically. Rhetorical features, such as logic, emotion, and the character of the writer are used to consider how a work induces others to cooperate. The definitions of rhetoric, and there are many, often have to do with the effect of the whole in relation to the parts, and understanding how people persuade us with rhetorical tools is probably one of the best things students can learn for both pleasure and survival. If we know how people influence people, we are less likely to be persuaded to do something against our will. The following analysis looks at how media persuades someone to believe beauty is what the media defines as beauty and asks us to consider that definition of beauty in terms of its consequences.

Assignment 3:
Rhetorical Analysis

You will write a rhetorical analysis of a print advertisement. Using material from our readings and work in class, you should consider both the elements of rhetoric such as audience, context, purpose, and genre, as well as the elements of visual rhetoric such as color, typeface, spatial relations, and use of images/text.

Advertisements: You may select one advertisement from print sources such as newspapers, magazines, or circulars. You may choose an ad from any point in print in the last five years; however, your analysis must allude to the time and culture in which the ad appeared. When you turn in your final draft, you must include a color copy or original of the print ad.

Purpose: This assignment provides an opportunity for you to closely examine a small part of the advertising that overwhelms our daily lives. This process is designed to help you learn how to recognize persuasion and rhetorical strategies used in persuasion.

Evaluation:

1. Ethos, Logos, and Pathos: Have you considered how each of these appeals functions to elicit a persuasive response? What might have been made this ad more persuasive?
2. Audience, Context, Purpose: Have you evaluated who this ad appeals to? What is the purpose of this ad? How does this ad fit within the cultural context?
3. Visual Rhetoric: Have you looked closely at the layout of the ad? How do the text and images work together to persuade? What could make this ad more visually persuasive?
4. Grammar/mechanics (10%: Is the paper edited well to eliminate errors in form, grammar, and spelling?

Audience: Write this with your ENGL 191 instructor as the intended audience.

Desired Outcomes

1. Experimentation with close reading and analysis – This is an opportunity for you to express what you think about why an ad is the way it is. However, this is academic writing and will require more than a shallow look at an advertisement in order to receive a passing grade.
1. Examination of rhetorical situations – This assignment provides an opportunity for you to examine various rhetorical situations and strategies of persuasion.

Arguments or critical essays

The basic pattern for a classic argument might be a discussion of the conflict, a segment explaining an opponent's perspective, your refutation of that point of view, and some call for action associated with your argument. A critical essay is a less formal approach to an argument in which the composer analyzes something and argues for or against what the other composer is arguing.

An argument asks you to take a position and to present your reasoning, supported by research, for taking that perspective on a topic. Although this seems simply a matter of finding information that supports a writer's thinking on a topic, a demonstration of "critically engaging information" will mean that the writer is also critical of his or her own position to a point. To simply begin with an attitude of "I am right and the rest are wrong" may work in a debate and is often accepted in editorials, but an academic argument must consider alternatives and you should find a way to include them in the paper.

Remember that in developing an argument you are picking something to write about that *reasonable people can and do disagree about*. Unless a writer is using a debate format in which there is a judge to decide who wins and loses, the academic argument is intended to show your line of reasoning and to give others reasons for agreeing with you. Arguments are about getting others to cooperate in doing something or in seeing a writer's point of view on a topic. What follows is an assignment for a critical essay.

Assignment 4:
Critical Essay

Audience: Academic

Purpose: To craft an argument about a text/movie, using the text/movie as your source of evidence.

Assignment Length: 1,000-1,500 words (roughly 3-4 pages)

Assignment: In this assignment, you will write a critical essay on one of the following:

- The movie *Groundhog Day*
- A piece from *Survive and Thrive Anthology*

You will develop a thesis: an argument — a central idea or interpretation — about the text. Using the artifact itself as your source of evidence, you will support your argument by describing its literary/cinematic devices. To support you in this task, you will use the double-entry journal as a tool for actively engaging with the text/movie.

Depending on which artifact you choose, you may also wish to annotate the text or movie. Your instructor may provide the script to the movie or anthology.

Some good composition thinkers believe that all compositions are critical essays. The idea is that we want to encourage critical thinking and the interpretation of information and the writings of others. Although our research and thinking leads us to be confident in our interpretations, composers must always recognize that their analysis and interpretation is an attempt to compose a response rather than a document that proves the Truth with a capital T.

Editor's Note

THINKING ALOUD

Here comes the building inspector. The experience of submitting your document or presentation for a grade is like completing a house and having a visit from the building inspector. Your grade is the inspector's best judgement about your success in building the house, not the plan, the materials, your skill at construction, or your standing as a human being. Simply, the judgement of a grade concerns your performance on the one project you submit and its success or failure according to the assignment. If the building inspector fails the project, he or she will give you the reasons for that assessment. Sometimes, depending on the policies of the class, you can fix those things for an amended assessment. In other words, check the syllabus for the policy on resubmissions. There are benefits and drawbacks to every variation on this policy — so, work with the policy. When you submit the first time, however, make sure you give it your best shot.

APPENDIX

Write in this book. Tear out the following pages. Be a hands-on analog user!

Most textbooks are fussy. The publishers want you to cover them in plastic, sanitize every page, and basically rent it, even if you paid full price, which can be anywhere from $80 to $150 as an average. (We know some cost more.) The idea for *Huskies Write* is that from the start you will not be selling it back, and we hope you will not want to. So, experience the real usefulness and thrill of real ownership. Stake your claim. Write in and on it. Underline and highlight. Doodle until you drool. Tear out the tear-out sheets that follow and use them as integral parts of the class and your experience.

Tear-out list

1. Invention to design prototype: Adapted from Jeremy Gutsche in *Exploiting Chaos*. Follow the directions on the tear out sheet. As you do consider the following: 1) Coming up with ideas is brainstorming with a purpose. Follow the six suggestions and you will find the experience rewarding. 2) Filtering is a matter of making choices about what seems most important to you in the context of your assignment.

2. A quick and dirty peer review: When you want to exchange papers or presentations for a review and to look for highlights, use this one. It makes a good class workshop as well.

3. Scavenger hunt: May be done in class or outside of class but are subject to time constraints. Apps for composition — The tear-out is simply a blank sheet with Apps for Composition on it. A scavenger hunt is a collection of apps you find around the web and the apps you use or could use for digital composition. The idea of a scavenger hunt is that you set a period of time when you and your classmates (competitors) see how much you can gather. Bring the hunt results back after the time period and see who got the most. Then make a list as a class of the top ten apps.

4. Things to do with an English major or minor

5. Participation, Influence, Respect

6. Commonly used Write Place Handouts - You will find the Write Place Handouts useful even if you think you don't need them. As tear-out sheets they are available for you to tear out and put with your notes for design, style workshops, or editing. In addition, if you know of someone struggling with any of these common challenges in a composition class, tear it out and give it to them as a gift.

   a) Effective Thesis Statements
   b) Comma Rules
   c) Rhetorical Analysis
   d) Suggested Structure for an Argument

Invention to Prototype Design

Follow the steps below and do them during a designated period of time in class or in a group meeting out of class:

1. Ideas! Ideas! Ideas!

Collect interesting possibilities. Brainstorming sessions have become too familiar and often tired excuses for what they were intended for. The following is an approach by Stanford University faculty and students that makes sense and gets things done. Remember to have one person in the group listing the ideas: When you generate ideas together defer judgment, encourage WILD ideas, go for volume, try to focus on one wild idea together at a time, headline ideas when you can (as in, "Great ideas come from letting judgment go right now), or springboard (any idea that gets people adding to it is a good idea to work with). Goal: Collect at least 30 ideas.

2. Synthesize and filter

During this phase use the ideas in 1., and filter them down to 10 or so ideas that most attract you, then rank those ideas by order of importance. Select your best 3 ideas.

3. Protoyping

Create mock diagrams, frameworks, physical mockups, slide shows, flow charts, or any other prototype designs for your document or presentation.

A Quick and Dirty Peer Review

Reviewers:

Use the following to give a peer response to your classmate's paper.

1. Ah Ha: a significant discovery
2. Reason: a point where its time for a good reason for what she or he is saying
3. Zinger: a "stylish" sentence or phrase
4. A Wavy line: a point in the paper he or she should rewrite, even though there might be something that is obviously wrong or not
5. A Straight Line: a part of the document where she or he needs help with a line of reasoning or a story line (You can't follow the progression.)

Writers:

Spend some time talking about what your peer reader found in your paper. In other words, it might not be enough to simply have them read the paper, mark something, and give it back. Part of the fun of writing is the opportunity to talk about it.

Apps for Composition Scavenger Hunt

1. During a specified period of time, collect as many apps that will help with composition for tablets and computers. The group or person who gets the most wins.

2. Have the class collect the apps, and spend some time inside or outside of class looking at them and, if possible, testing them.

3. In the class, make a list of the 10 best apps for composing and where they may be found. (It is a good idea actually to make two lists: free apps and apps that you pay for.)

Notes:

Things to Do with an English Major or Minor, and Your Career

(Time Period: 60 to 90 minutes)

- Make a list of your top three career interests.

- Do digital research to determine the relationship of a possible English major or minor that works with your interests. Hint: If you are stuck, consider the career skills for the Twenty-first Century in Chapter 1, page 20.

- Share your findings in class

Career interests	English major or minor

Participation, Influence, Respect

How do you participate in class, on campus, and in the community?

How do you have influence in your class, on campus, in the community? Who listens and takes what you have to say into account — classmates, faculty, staff, members of the wider community?

How do you receive and show respect? Consider classmates, faculty, SCSU, and the wider community. (Example: Talk with someone keeping the grounds for SCSU and thank them for what they are doing.)

Tear out and post your answers where you can see it often. You may use this tear-out or create a one-page presentation.

—

Write Place Handout: Effective Thesis Statements

A Thesis Statement is a sentence(s) that explicitly identifies the purpose of the paper or previews its main ideas.

1. Determine what type of paper you are writing and what type of thesis statement is needed.

   - Analytical paper: breaks down an issue or idea into component parts, evaluates the issue or idea, and presents this breakdown and evaluation to the audience.
   - Expository paper: explains something to the audience
   - Argumentative paper: makes a claim about a topic and justifies claim with specific evidence or arguments. The goal is to persuade the audience that the claim is trued based on evidence and arguments provide.

   If you are writing a paper that does not fall under one of these categories, a thesis statement found in the first paragraph might still be helpful to the reader.

2. Thesis statements should be specific. Cover only what you will be discussing in the paper and support the claim with exact evidence.

3. The thesis statement is usually found at the end of the first paragraph of a paper.

4. The topic of a paper may change as it is written, so one may need to revise the thesis statement to reflect what is being discussed in the paper.

- Examples -

Example of an analytical thesis statement:
An analysis of the college admission process reveals one challenge facing counselors: accepting students with high test scores or students with strong extracurricular backgrounds.

Example of an expository thesis statement:
The life of a typical college student is characterized by time spent studying, attending class, and socializing with peers.

Example of an argumentative thesis statement:
High school graduates should be required to take a year off to pursue community service projects before entering college in order to increase their maturity and global awareness.

A thesis statement is an assertion:
People are poisoning the environment with chemicals merely to keep their lawns clean.

A thesis statement takes a stand:
Solving our environmental problems is more difficult than many environmentalists believe.

A thesis statement is a main idea, not the title of a paper.
Continuing changes in the Social Security System makes it almost impossible to plan intelligently for one's retirement.

A thesis statement is narrow, rather than broad.
The primary problem of the American steel industry is the lack of funds to renovate outdated plants and equipment.

A thesis statement is specific, rather than vague or general.
Hemingway's stories helped to create a new prose style by employing extensive dialogue, shorter sentences, and strong Anglo-Saxon words.

A thesis statement has one main point rather than several main points.
Stephan Hawking's physical disability has not prevented him from becoming a world renowned physicist.

You can revise a thesis statement during the writing of your paper. Writers often discover what their real purpose and/or point of the paper is revealed in the process of putting their thoughts into words and then reading what they have written.

Copyright 2013 The Write Place
Kate Hysjulien Hogue

Use a comma...

1. **before a coordinating conjunction (and, or, but, nor, yet, for, so) that separates two independent clauses:**

    She is a very smart young lady, but sometimes she cannot see what is right in front of her.

    David is really good at soccer, and he is an excellent student as well.

2. **after an introductory word, phrase or clause that comes before a main clause:**

    However, I find the curtains in Mrs. Schirel's house to be tacky and distracting.

    Because we were having so many computer problems, everyone in the lab lost their papers.

    Clearly, Amy doesn't know how to tie her shoes.

    If you get this last question right, you will win $1,000,000; if you get it wrong, you walk away with nothing.

3. **around words, phrases and clauses in the middle of a sentence when they are not essential to the meaning of the sentence:**

    My best friend, Marissa, took me out to dinner for my birthday.

    Kanye West, a famous performer, took a big risk during the 2009 VMA awards.

4. **between items in a series:**

    She broke the chair, the fridge, the toaster and my muffin pan!

    If she starts paying attention in class, gets her work in on time and does some extra credit, she might be able to pass.

5. **before and after a quotation within a sentence:**

    "There are many strange things in the world," he said, "I think your brother is one of them."

    She stood on top of the table and yelled, "We're not gonna take it!"

6. **before an afterthought:**

    She was awesome, especially when she made jokes.

7. **to set off geographical names, items in date and professional titles:**

    He was from Atlanta, Georgia.

    My dog died on March 14th, 1990, when he fell into the river.'

    I will never forget my old address, 354, 6th Ave South, St. Joseph, New Mexico.

Copyright 2013 The Write Place
Last Revised by Caitlin Hites

Write Place Handout: Rhetorical Analysis

Context
- What motivated the author to choose this particular subject?
- What has already been mentioned about the subject in the past?

Purpose
- What does the author want the readers to be able to do, think, feel, or decide?

Audience
- Who are the intended audience and what are their expectations?

Exigency
- The sense of need or urgency for an argument.
- The appropriateness of a particular argument for a particular, time, place, and audience.

Style
- What is the style of the piece? Formal? Informal? Academic?
- Is the piece serious? Humorous? Satirical? Critical? Explanatory?

Rhetorical Analysis of Content
- What kinds of evidence — facts, statistics, anecdotes — does the author use?
- How does the author use supporting evidence to appeal to the reader?
- Are these appeals logical and rational? Emotional? A combination of the two?
- What does the selection of details tell you about the author's assumption of the knowledge and experience of the audience?

Rhetorical Analysis of Organization
- How does the organization of the text help fulfill its purpose?
- What cueing devices are used to emphasize important points and to guide the reader through the essay? Do visual clues — headings, spacing, listing — help organize the text for the reader, or emphasize (or de-emphasize) certain points?
- Is the information clustered or segmented in a way meaningful to readers and compatible with purpose? Does clustering of information follow established patterns (e.g., classification, description, comparison, contrast, problem/

solution, and so on)?

Rhetorical Analysis of Expression
- How does the language of the text help the text fulfill its purpose for the readers?
- How do the following uses of language influence the text?
    1. concrete versus abstract words
    2. level of technicality
    3. formality (e.g., highly formal, use of slang) Be specific.

- How does the author use language to establish a certain tone? Be specific.
- What kinds of sentences does the author use? Simple, complex? Long, short, medium? Varied? Why? Does the author use topic sentences or forecasting statements to guide readers? Give examples.

Classical Rhetorical Appeals
Rhetorical appeals are persuasive strategies used by an author.

- *Ethos:* Ethos is the way in which an author establishes credibility. This can be done by stating qualifications in the field, by using examples and quoted or paraphrased information from reputable sources, demonstrating fairness, and by displaying expertise about the subject.

- *Logos:* Logos is the use of factual information to promote logical decision-making by the audience.

- *Pathos:* Pathos is the way in which the author appeals to the emotions of the audience. This can be accomplished by using emotional language, anecdotes, some hypothetical examples, or sensory description.

Copyright 2013 The Write Place
Revised by Kristin Henderson

Model Paper: Argumentative Research Paper

Cheyenne Baca
Mr. Douglas LeBlanc
ENGL 191
April 17, 2013

The International Adoption Crisis

Many countries have been banning international adoptions in the past fifteen years. One common reason for them doing so is because there have been cases where parents have been paid to give up their babies for adoption instead of giving them up freely. Another reason is because there have been cases where young children and babies have been stolen from their homes and illegally adopted in foreign countries. Most of the time, the adoptive parents do not even know that their child has been stolen from another family. A third reason is because there have been children who after adoption have been subjected to domestic servitude or child prostitution. However, banning international adoptions has prevented many truly orphaned or given up children from going into good homes. My essay, then, after examining different sources such as government documents and scholarly articles, will hopefully show that international adoption does not have to be banned in order to prevent these crimes.

A debatable thesis that shows your plan of action; great!

In 2003, my family went through the process of adopting two children with special needs from India. Josy and Sanjay, ages 3 and 2 ½ respectively, both had Beta Thalassemia Major, a blood condition which prevents them from reproducing their own red blood cells. In the orphanage, they were not getting the proper care for their condition, and if they had not been adopted, they would have died. Because they are a part of our family now, they are able to get the care they need to stay alive and healthy. Sadly, as international adoptions are declining, there are many children like my younger siblings who are being forced to stay in unsuitable conditions.

Good. Here you are connecting with your readers and increasing your persuasive ability through ETHOS.

There are those people who are very much against international adoption. Baroness Emma Nicholson, who was a former European Parliament Rapporteur for Romania, succeeded in helping to bring about Romania's non-international adoption law. Nicholson stated in her article "Red Light on Human Traffic" that "[c]hildren exported abroad – often against their will – are often subjected to paedophilia, child prostitution or domestic servitude" (par. 3). However, on reading the article one finds very little concrete evidence. Most of the article seems to be mainly playing upon the reader's emotions, with words such as "horrific" and "disastrous" and phrases such as "torn from their families." It is meant to make readers feel that the situation in Romania was terrible, when in fact, the problem was greatly exaggerated. To add evidence to her point, Nicholson cites a case where two Romanian girls in an institution were adopted by two Italian families "against their wishes" and were going to be sent away until the European court of human rights overruled the Romanian court's decision that the girls were to be sent away. However, Richard Carlson, in the footnotes of his essay "Seeking the Better Interests of Children with a new International Law of Adoption" gives evidence that the case wasn't so simple. He states:

While you give credit to this source here, you forgot to add the article to your Works Cited. So check for this during the proofreading process.

Good! You are getting inside the argument and refuting it.

> According to the court, Italian couples obtained adoption decrees for Florentina and Marina in September 2000. However, over the next three years, the children's home (referenced herein as the "CEPSB") where Florentina and Marina resided in Romania

successfully resisted transferring custody to the adoptive parents, sometimes hiding the children from police, and thereby preventing any contact between the children and adoptive parents over an extended period of time. Despite over three years of litigation between the adoptive parents and CEPSB, there does not appear to have been any evidence or allegation that the childrens' birth families were resisting the adoption or that the adoption decrees were procured by fraud or bribery. (Endnote 40)

Looking at this evidence, it appears that Nicholson was willfully misinterpreting the facts in order to fit it in with her own agenda – to ban international adoption in Romania. She completely ignores the fact that the two girls were sometimes hidden from the police by their institution, and instead includes only those parts of the case that fit with what she wanted to say. It is true that the two girls were found to have said that they did not want to leave CEPSB or be adopted by people that they did not know. It was for this reason the court overruled the adoption, not any suspicious activity within the adoption proceedings, as Nicholson was implying. The court also found that "Romania had violated the adoptive parents' rights by disrupting the adoptions, and it awarded damages in favor of the adoptive parents" (Endnote 40).

Nicholson was not the only one who brought about the new law, however. Romania, after requesting to join the European Union, was reprimanded by them on their history of corrupt adoptions. Romania put a temporary freeze on all adoptions in order to take some time to investigate their pending international adoptions, but shortly after their acceptance into the Union they put the permanent ban in place. But, as Molly S. Marx states,

> Romania's adoption legislation removes a vital safeguard that previously provided homes for unwanted children and leaves these children in the inadequate care of the State. The Romanian government can promote and accomplish the goals of Law 272 and Law 273 without taking the drastic measure of outlawing international adoptions. The two goals are not mutually exclusive. (390)

The people who are against international adoption argue that they are working for the best interests of the child. But if a child is needlessly kept in an orphanage or foster home in poor conditions, when they could have a loving home through international adoption, how is that in the best interests of the child? It is true that there are cases where children are taken from families or bribed away, and that people who do this are usually out to make a profit. But that is no reason why international adoption as a whole should be considered corrupt.

In the Orange County Register, there is an article on a woman who had her child stolen from her. In March of 2007 in Guatemala, Ana Escobar was tending the small shoe store owned by her family when she was locked in a storage room by a gunman. When she finally got free she found that her 6-month-old baby girl, Esther, was stolen. Devastated, she searched for over a year in orphanages and hospitals, and looking at every little child on the street to see if they might resemble her missing daughter. Finally, she found her daughter by chance in the arms of a foster mother, weeks away from being handed over to a couple in Indiana. The authorities, on obtaining proof that Esther was indeed Escobar's daughter, immediately arrested the people who had been involved in putting the child up for adoption—the woman listed as the birth mother, the foster mother, the lawyer brokering the adoption, a doctor, and the lawyer representing the couple from Indiana. According to the Orange County Register, authorities had long suspected that a number of the babies adopted each year from Guatemala were stolen and "sold to baby brokers who worked with doctors and lawyers to create false identities for the children" (Llorca, par.10).

Such proceedings are horrible to think about — that there are people who will create

As noted, you are doing a good job of getting inside the other side and arguing with it. However, you can increase your effect here by adding that such fear is natural.

Good choice of using a quote here. Sometimes it is best to summarize, but the strength of these words make them ideal for a direct quote.

Nice use of rhetorical question. It forces your readers to seek for an answer.

a false identity for a child in order for the adoption to look good, all to make money off of it. Article 11 of the Hague Convention in 2000 on Protection of Children and Cooperation in Respect of Intercountry Adoption states that an accredited body performing central authority—discharging the duties imposed by the Convention—must "(a) pursue non-profit objectives according to conditions set by the State of accreditation; (b) be directed and staffed by persons qualified by their ethical standards and by training or experience to work in the field of intercountry adoption; and (c) be supervised by the competent authorities of the State of accreditation" (5). It is clear that there are some who are not following these rules. Thus, I would like to suggest stronger regulations in international adoption, such as extensive background checks on every person who is involved in the adoption process of a child. This would help ensure that the proceedings are legal—or help prove them illegal. For instance, a seemingly good document that was drawn up by a lawyer who has had cases of misconduct, or who is working with people who are deceiving him.

It is good that you admit the other side in the paragraph above with the use of a powerful anecdote. Then, in this paragraph here, you help your readers see where the true blame lies. Well done.

There have already been steps taken to ensure that these things such as child stealing do not happen. Jo Daugherty Bailey says in her essay that "concerns regarding "irregularities" in Vietnam, such as reports of payments by service providers to orphanage directors for referrals of children for international adoption, recently led U.S. Citizenship and Immigration Services to initiate a requirement of DNA testing to facilitate confirmation of the orphan status of children to be adopted" (170). With this requirement in place, it will be harder for criminals to steal a child and pretend that it is orphaned, or pass it off as another woman's baby, as was the case with Ana Escobar's child.

Article 19 of the Hague Convention states that "the central authorities of both States ensure that the transfer [of the child to their new country] occurs in secure and appropriate circumstances and, when possible, accompanied by the adoptive or prospective adopted parents" (6). I believe that the adoptive parents should always accompany the transfer, along with an appropriate authority figure. I would also suggest that the adoptive family be checked up on a few times in the first few weeks. These suggestions would help to decrease the fear of bad conduct on the way over, as well as the fear of abuse or domestic servitude within the first few weeks.

You open this paragraph with a quote and then proceed to draw out the significance in your own words, making it relevant. This is important to effective research writing.

There are many parts of the Hague Convention which would help to decrease the adoption crimes going on. However, it is not a perfect document. Kayla Webley, in her essay, quotes lawyer Kelly Ensslin when she says, ""The Hague is a good idea in theory. But it's more of a guidebook than an instruction manual. Many countries lack the infrastructure to implement the legislation and uniform systems it requires'" (par. 11). There are many poor countries that cannot afford to have a central authority to process adoptions. Also, the Hague convention has done more to harm the international adoption cause than to help it, with countries who are a part of the convention banning international adoptions, or jumping in without being properly prepared.

Good. By admitting some flaws in the system you actually increase your ETHOS.

However, not every adoption is filled with abuse, secrecy, and lies. For every adoption which is a fraud, there are many more that are perfectly good, and that give children good homes with loving families. Banning international adoption is not the answer. Although it does prevent many children from being sold to other countries, it also prevents children, especially in the poorer countries that cannot afford to adopt many of their own children, from going to homes where they will be loved. I believe that what we need is stronger rules and closer regulation to help decrease the adoption frauds. Carlson says it very well at the end of his essay. He states:

By putting a semicolon at the end of the word "essay," you can remove the "He states:"

"The answer is careful regulation, not prohibition. Indeed, regulation designed to prevent real abuse is as necessary in the intercountry arena as it is in domestic adoption, but too much regulation can backfire. Overregulation will strand thousands of children in institutions, raise costs beyond the reach of many prospective adopters, and drive other prospective adopters into nations where costs are low and adoptions are "possible" but legal protection for any of the parties is weak. The "right" level of regulation will be no guarantee that every child's adoptive placement will be perfect, ideal, or even lawful. Adoption is no more capable of perfection than any other worthy child welfare policy. However, the benefits that adoption offers, and the many children who would almost certainly benefit by adoption, make it a policy that deserves our efforts. (778)

This large block quote may be a bit long for tacking on at the end of the essay. However, this highlighted part is a magnificent argument. I would therefore try to trim the block quote down some. Your readers will take more from it that way.

Works Cited

Bailey, Jo Daugherty. "Expectations of the Consequences of New International Adoption Policy in the U.S." Journal of Sociology and Social Welfare 36.2 (2009): 169-182. Web.

Carlson, Richard. "Seeking the Better Interests of Children with a New International Law of Adoption." New York Law School Law Review 55.3 (2010): 734-779. Web.

Llorca, Juan Carlos. "Her Baby Was Stolen and Put Up for Adoption." Orange County Register. Orange County Register, 1 Aug. 2008. Web.

Marx, Molly S. "Whose Best Interests Does it Really Serve? A Critical Examination of Romania's Recent Self-Serving International Adoption Policies." International Law Review 21.1 (2007): 373-412. Web.

United States Congress. Senate Executive Reports, Nos. 14-27. Washington: United States Government Printing Office, 2002. Print.

Webley, Kayla. "The Baby Deficit." Time 181.2 (2013): 34-39. Web.

Cheyenne,

Excellent job on this argumentative research paper! You write clearly, you bring in excellent primary and secondary sources, and you offer a critical analysis of them. A model paper. See comments throughout.

Grade: A

Outcome criteria	5 Exemplary	4 Exceeds	3 Meets	2 Inadequate	1 Fails to meet	Score
Structure of written work	Form and structure of written work clearly and effectively develop focused insight, carry out writer's purpose, and goes beyond just following conventions of the genre.	Written work clearly and effectively carries out writer's purpose, with strong thesis & strong beginning, development, and conclusion. Effective paragraphing and transitions.	Written work has clear and appropriate thesis, beginning, development and conclusion. Paragraphing and transitions are clear and appropriate.	Written work has weak beginning, development, and conclusion. Paragraphing and transitions are also deficient. Form or genre of work is not clearly established.	Organizational structure and paragraphing have serious and persistent errors. Form or genre of the work does not fit the assignment.	
Critical thinking achieved	Writer establishes vision of her/his own; shows independence of thought in using sources to produce knowledge; finds balance or synthesis among opposing or alternative views. See "Exceeds."	Length of written work provides in-depth coverage of topic, and supports assertions with evidence. Writer uses research materials strategically in analyzing and producing knowledge and responds effectively to opposing views.	Length of the written work is adequate to cover the topic, and assertions are supported by evidence. Good, methodical survey of sources available.	Written work does not adequately cover the topic, and assertions are weakly supported by evidence.	Written work does not cover the assigned topic, and assertions are not supported by evidence.	
Rhetorical competence and mechanics	Writer establishes a distinctive or professional voice and uses alternative viewpoints or worldviews to frame an argument or draw implications. See "Exceeds."	Style appropriate to audience; shows awareness of audience. Written work has no major errors in word selection and use, sentence structure, spelling, punctuation, and grammar. Correct documentation.	Written work is relatively free of errors in word selection and use, sentence structure, spelling, punctuation, and grammar. Documents sources adequately.	Written work has several major errors in word selection and use, sentence structure, spelling, punctuation, and grammar. Work does not document sources adequately.	Written work has serious and persistent errors in word selection and use, sentence structure, spelling, punctuation, and grammar. Sources lack documentation	
Total						

Illustrations

Text

AUTOGRAPHS

AUTOGRAPHS

AUTOGRAPHS